HOW NO

MW01256627

"*How Nonviolence Prot.*
by the privileged through ideological nonviolence and challenges white middle class activists to question if they are truly committed to solidarity with oppressed peoples."
—Jason Lydon, Congregational Director, Community Church of Boston

"Thoroughly-researched and extremely well-argued, *How Nonviolence Protects the State* is a potent antidote to the insufferably self-serving sanctimony which has for far too long been able to pass itself off as a 'principled opposition' in the United States."
—Ward Churchill, author, *Pacifism as Pathology*

"I am deeply grateful to Peter Gelderloos for having the courage to show the cult of pacifism for what it is: a racist, patriarchal ally of state power. *How Nonviolence Protects the State* is a necessary book on a necessary subject: how shall we resist."
—Derrick Jensen, author, *A Language Older Than Words*

"*How Nonviolence Protects the State* makes a strong argument for the diversity of tactics, while illuminating how the ideology of pacifism leads us not to social justice, but rather, the peace one finds in cemeteries. A must read."
—Ann Hansen, author, *Direct Action: Memoirs of an Urban Guerilla*

"It will be a shame if *How Nonviolence Protects the State* isn't read and discussed by people who disagree with it. If it isn't, that will prove its central thesis—that pacifism retains its hegemony in some circles only because people refuse to acknowledge the possibility of other approaches to social change."
—CrimethInc. Ex-Workers' Collective

HOW NONVIOLENCE PROTECTS THE STATE

HOW NONVIOLENCE PROTECTS THE STATE

PETER GELDERLOOS

SOUTH END PRESS
CAMBRIDGE, MASSACHUSETTS

Cover design by Design Action Collective
Cover photographs: Josh Reynolds, www.joshreynoldsphoto.com
Text design by Alexander Dwinell, South End Press collective
Printed in Canada by union labor on acid-free paper.

Library of Congress Cataloging-in-Publication Data

Gelderloos, Peter.
  How nonviolence protects the state / Peter Gelderloos.
      p. cm.
  Includes bibliographical references and index.
  ISBN 978-0-89608-772-9
  1. Nonviolence. I. Title.

HM1281.G45 2007
303.6--dc22

                                              2007000848

South End Press
7 Brookline Street #1
Cambridge, MA 02139-4146
www.southendpress.org

        11 10 09 08 07   1 2 3 4 5 6 7 8

And they say that the beauty's in the streets
but when I look around it seems more like defeat

—Defiance Ohio

This book is dedicated to Sue Daniels (1960–2004), a brilliant ecologist, bold feminist, passionate anarchist, and beautiful and caring human being who nurtured and challenged everyone around her. Your bravery and wisdom continue to inspire me, and in that way your spirit remains indomitable...

...and to Greg Michael (1961–2006), who embodied health, as a wholeness of being and an indefatigable quest against the poisons of our world, even in the unhealthiest of circumstances. From a bag of raisins stolen from the prison kitchen to the unfolding of memory on a mountaintop, the gifts you have given me are a salve and a weapon, and they will stay with me until the last prison is a pile of rubble.

Special thanks to Megan, Patrick, Carl, Gopal, and Sue D. for proofreading or giving me feedback, and to Sue F., James, Iris, Marc, Edi, Alexander, Jessica, Esther, and everyone who came to the workshops for criticism valuable to this second edition.

Table of Contents

i

INTRODUCTION

In August 2004, at the North American Anarchist Convergence in Athens, Ohio, I participated in a panel discussing the topic of nonviolence versus violence. Predictably, the discussion turned into an unproductive and competitive debate. I had hoped that each panelist would be given a substantial amount of time to speak in order to present our ideas in depth and to limit the likely alternative of a back-and-forth volley of clichéd arguments. But the facilitator, who was also a conference organizer, and on top of that a panelist, decided against this approach.

Because of the hegemony advocates of nonviolence exert, criticisms of nonviolence are excluded from the major periodicals, alternative media, and other forums accessed by anti-authoritarians.[1] Nonviolence is maintained as an article of faith, and as a key to full inclusion within the movement. Anti-authoritarians and anti-capitalists who suggest or practice militancy suddenly find themselves abandoned by the same pacifists they've just marched with at the latest protest. Once isolated, militants lose access to resources, and they lose protection from being scapegoated by the media or criminalized by the government. Within these dynamics caused by the knee-jerk isolation of those who do not conform to nonviolence, there is no possibility for a healthy or critical discourse to evaluate our chosen strategies.

In my experience, most people who are becoming involved with radical movements have never heard good arguments, or even bad ones, against nonviolence. This is true even when they already know a great deal about other movement issues. Instead, they tend to be acquainted with the aura of taboo that shrouds militants; to have internalized the fear and disdain the corporate media reserve for people willing to actually fight against capitalism and the state; and to have confused the isolation imposed on militants with some self-imposed isolation that must be inherent in militancy. Most proponents of nonviolence with whom I have discussed these issues, and these have been many, approached the conversation like it was a foregone conclusion that the use of violence in social movements was both wrong and self-defeating (at least if it occurred anywhere within 1,000 miles of them). On the contrary, there are a great many solid arguments against nonviolence that pacifists have simply failed to answer in their literature.

This book will show that nonviolence, in its current manifestations, is based on falsified histories of struggle. It has implicit and explicit connections to white people's manipulations of the struggles of people of color. Its methods are wrapped in authoritarian dynamics, and its results are harnessed to meet government objectives over popular objectives. It masks and even encourages patriarchal assumptions and power dynamics. Its strategic options invariably lead to dead ends. And its practitioners delude themselves on a number of key points.

Given these conclusions, if our movements are to have any possibility of destroying oppressive systems such as capitalism and white supremacy and building a free and healthy world, we must spread these criticisms and end the stranglehold of nonviolence over discourse while developing more effective forms of struggle.

We might say that the purpose of a conversation is to persuade and be persuaded, while the purpose of a debate is to win, and thus silence your opponent. One of the first steps to success in any debate is to control the terminology to give oneself the advantage and put one's opponents at a disadvantage. This is exactly what pacifists have done in phrasing the disagreement as *nonviolence versus violence*. Critics of nonviolence typically use this dichotomy, with which most of us fundamentally disagree, and push to expand the boundaries of nonviolence so that tactics we support, such as property destruction, may be accepted within a nonviolent framework, indicating how disempowered and delegitimized we are.

I know of no activist, revolutionary, or theorist relevant to the movement today who advocates only the use of violent tactics and opposes any usage of tactics that could not be called violent. We are advocates of a *diversity of tactics*, meaning effective combinations drawn from a full range of tactics that might lead to liberation from all the components of this oppressive system: white supremacy, patriarchy, capitalism, and the state. We believe that tactics should be chosen to fit the particular situation, not drawn from a preconceived moral code. We also tend to believe that means are reflected in the ends, and would not want to act in a way that invariably would lead to dictatorship or some other form of society that does not respect life and freedom. As such, we can more accurately be described as proponents of revolutionary or militant activism than as proponents of violence.[2]

I will refer to proponents of nonviolence by their chosen nomenclature, as nonviolent activists or, interchangeably, pacifists. Many practitioners of such prefer one term or the other, and some even make a distinction between the two, but in my experience the distinctions are not consistent from one person to the next. Most importantly, pacifists/nonviolent activists themselves tend to collaborate regardless of their chosen term, so the difference in labels is not important to the considerations of this book. Broadly, by using the term *pacifism* or *nonviolence*, they designate a way of life or a method of social activism that avoids, transforms, or excludes violence while attempting to change society to create a more peaceful and free world.

At this point it might help to clearly define *violence*, but one of the critical arguments of this book is that *violence* cannot be clearly defined. I should also clarify a few other terms that pop up frequently. The word *radical* I use literally, to mean a critique, action, or person that goes to the *roots* of a particular problem rather than focusing on the superficial solutions placed on the table by the prejudices and powers of the day. The word is not a synonym for *extreme* or *extremist*, much as the media would have us believe it is, through ignorance or design. (Similarly, in case anyone is still unclear: an anarchist is not someone who favors chaos but someone who favors the total liberation of the world through the abolition of capitalism, government, and all other forms of oppressive authority, to be replaced by any number of other social arrangements, proven or utopian.) On the other hand, I do not use the word *revolution* literally, to mean the overthrow of current rulers by a new set of rulers (which would make *anti-authoritarian revolution* an oxymoron), but only to mean a social upheaval with widespread transformative effects. I use this word only because it has such long-standing favorable connotations, and because the more accurate alternative, *liberation*, is clumsy in its adjectival forms.

To reemphasize a crucial distinction: the criticisms in this book are not aimed at specific actions that do not exemplify violent behavior, such as a vigil that remains peaceful, nor are they aimed at individual activists who choose to dedicate themselves to noncombative work, such as healing or building strong community relationships. When I talk about pacifists and advocates of nonviolence, I am referring to those who would impose their ideology across the entire movement and dissuade other activists from militancy (including the use of violence), or who would not support other activists solely because of their militancy. Likewise, an ideal revolutionary activist would not be one who obsessively focuses on fighting cops or engaging in clandestine acts of sabotage, but one who embraces and supports these activities, where effective, as one portion of a broad range of actions needed to overthrow the state and build a better world.

Though I focus on debunking pacifism in service of revolutionary goals, in this book I include quotes from pacifists working for limited reforms in addition to quotes from people working for total social transformation. At first, this may seem like I am building a straw-man argument; however, I include the words or actions of reformist pacifists only in reference to campaigns where they worked together closely with revolutionary pacifists and the quoted material has relevance to all involved, or in reference to social struggles cited as examples proving the effectiveness of nonviolence in achieving revolutionary ends. It is difficult to distinguish between revolutionary and non-revolutionary pacifists, because they themselves tend not to make that distinction in the course of their activity—they work together, attend protests together, and frequently use the same tactics at the same actions. Because shared commitment to nonviolence, and not shared commitment to a revolutionary goal, is the chief criterion for nonviolent activists in deciding whom to work with, those are the boundaries I will use in defining these criticisms.

I could spend plenty of time talking about the failures of nonviolence. Instead, it may be more useful to talk about the successes of nonviolence. Pacifism would hardly be attractive to its supporters if the ideology had produced no historical victories. Typical examples are the independence of India from British colonial rule, caps on the nuclear arms race, the civil rights movement of the 1960s, and the peace movement during the war against Vietnam.[1] And though they have not yet been hailed as a victory, the massive protests in 2003 against the US invasion of Iraq have been much applauded by nonviolent activists.[2]

NONVIOLENCE IS INEFFECTIVE

There is a pattern to the historical manipulation and whitewashing evident in every single victory claimed by nonviolent activists. The pacifist position requires that success must be attributable to pacifist tactics and pacifist tactics alone, whereas the rest of us believe that change comes from the whole spectrum of tactics present in any revolutionary situation, provided they are deployed effectively. Because no major social conflict exhibits a uniformity of tactics and ideologies, which is to say that all such conflicts exhibit pacifist tactics and decidedly nonpacifist tactics, pacifists have to erase the history that disagrees with them or, alternately, blame their failures on the contemporary presence of violent struggle.[3]

In India, the story goes, people under the leadership of Gandhi built up a massive nonviolent movement over decades and engaged in protest, noncooperation, economic boycotts, and exemplary hunger strikes and acts of disobedience to make British imperialism unworkable. They suffered massacres and responded with a couple of riots, but, on the whole, the movement was nonviolent and, after persevering for decades, the Indian people won their independence, providing an undeniable hallmark of pacifist victory. The actual history is more complicated, in that many violent pressures also informed the British decision to withdraw. The British had lost the ability to maintain colonial power after losing millions of troops and a great deal of other resources during two extremely violent world wars, the second of which especially devastated the "mother country." The armed struggles of Arab and Jewish militants in Palestine from 1945 to 1948 further weakened the British Empire, and presented a clear threat that the Indians might give up civil disobedience and take up arms en masse if ignored for long enough; this cannot be excluded as a factor in the decision of the British to relinquish direct colonial administration.

We realize this threat to be even more direct when we understand that the pacifist history of India's independence movement is a selective and incomplete picture—nonviolence was not universal in India. Resistance to British colonialism included enough militancy that the Gandhian method can be viewed most accurately as one of several competing forms of popular resistance. As part of a disturbingly universal pattern, pacifists white out those other forms of resistance and help propagate the false history that Gandhi and his disciples were the lone masthead and rudder of Indian resistance. Ignored are important militant leaders such as Chandrasekhar Azad,[4] who fought in armed struggle against the British colonizers, and revolutionaries such as Bhagat Singh, who won mass support for bombings and assassinations as part of a struggle to accomplish the "overthrow of both foreign and Indian capitalism."[5] The pacifist history of India's struggle cannot make any sense of the fact that Subhas Chandra Bose, the militant candidate, was twice elected president of the Indian National Congress, in 1938 and 1939.[6] While Gandhi was perhaps the most singularly influential and popular figure in India's independence struggle, the leadership position he assumed did not always enjoy the consistent backing of the masses. Gandhi lost so much support from Indians when he "called off the movement" after the 1922 riot that when the British locked him up afterwards, "not a ripple of protest arose in India at his arrest."[7] Significantly, history remembers Gandhi above all others not because he represented the unanimous voice of India, but because of all the attention he was given by the British press and the prominence he received from being included in important negotiations with the British colonial government. When we remember that history is written by the victors, another layer of the myth of Indian independence comes unraveled.

The sorriest aspect of pacifists' claim that the independence of India is a victory for nonviolence is that this claim plays directly into the historical fabrication carried out in the interests of the white-supremacist, imperialist states that colonized the Global South. The liberation movement in India failed. The British were not forced to quit India. Rather, they chose to transfer the territory from direct colonial rule to neocolonial rule.[8] What kind of victory allows the losing side to dictate the time and manner of the victors' ascendancy? The British authored the new constitution and turned power over to handpicked successors. They fanned the flames of religious and ethnic separatism so that India would be divided against itself, prevented from gaining peace and prosperity, and dependent on military aid and other support from Euro/American states.[9] India is still exploited by Euro/ American corporations (though several new Indian corporations, mostly subsidiaries, have joined in the pillaging), and still provides resources and markets for the imperialist states. In many ways the poverty of its people has deepened and the exploitation has become more efficient. Independence from colonial rule has given India more autonomy in a few areas, and it has certainly allowed a handful of Indians to sit in the seats of power, but the exploitation and the commoditization of the commons and of culture have deepened. Moreover, India lost a clear opportunity for meaningful liberation from an easily recognizable foreign oppressor. Any liberation movement now would have to go up against the confounding dynamics of nationalism and ethnic/religious rivalry in order to abolish a domestic capitalism and government that are far more developed. On balance, the independence movement proves to have failed.

The claim of a pacifist victory in capping the nuclear arms race is somewhat bizarre. Once again, the movement was not exclusively nonviolent; it included groups that carried out a number of bombings and other acts of sabotage or guerrilla warfare.[10] And, again, the victory is a dubious one. The much-ignored nonproliferation treaties only came after the arms race had already been won, with the US as undisputed nuclear hegemon in possession of more nuclear weapons than was even practical or useful. And it seems clear that proliferation continues as needed, currently in the form of tactical nuke development and a new wave of proposed nuclear power facilities. Really, the entire issue seems to have been settled more as a matter of internal policy within the government than as a conflict between a social movement and a government. Chernobyl and several near meltdowns in the US showed that nuclear energy (a necessary component of nuclear arms development) was something of a liability, and it doesn't take a protestor to question the usefulness, even to a government bent on conquering the world, of diverting staggering resources toward nuclear proliferation when you already have enough bombs to blow up the entire planet, and every single war and covert action since 1945 has been fought with other technologies.

The US civil rights movement is one of the most important episodes in the pacifist history. Across the world, people see it as an example of nonviolent victory. But, like the other examples discussed here, it was neither a victory nor nonviolent. The movement was successful in ending de jure segregation and expanding the minuscule black petty bourgeoisie, but these were not the only demands of the majority of movement participants.[11] They wanted full political and economic equality, and many also wanted black liberation in the form of black nationalism, black intercommunalism, or some other independence from white imperialism. None of these demands were met—not equality, and certainly not liberation.

People of color still have lower average incomes, poorer access to housing and health care, and poorer health than white people. De facto segregation still exists.[12] Political equality is also lacking. Millions of voters, most of them black, are disenfranchised (from voting for white candidates in a white political system that reflects a white culture) when it is convenient to ruling interests, and only four black senators have served since Reconstruction.[13] Other races have also been missed by the mythical fruits of civil rights. Latino and Asian immigrants are especially vulnerable to abuse, deportation, denial of social services they pay taxes for, and toxic and backbreaking labor in sweatshops or as migrant agricultural laborers. Muslims and Arabs are taking the brunt of the post–September 11 repression, while a society that has anointed itself "color-blind" evinces nary a twinge of hypocrisy. Native peoples are kept so low on the socioeconomic ladder as to remain invisible, except for the occasional symbolic manifestation of US multiculturalism—the stereotyped sporting mascot or hula-girl doll that obscures the reality of actual indigenous people.

The common projection (primarily by white progressives, pacifists, educators, historians, and government officials) is that the movement against racial oppression in the United States was primarily nonviolent. On the contrary, though pacifist groups such as Martin Luther King Jr.'s Southern Christian Leadership Conference (SCLC) had considerable power and influence, popular support within the movement, especially among poor black people, increasingly gravitated toward militant revolutionary groups such as the Black Panther Party.[14] According to a 1970 Harris poll, 66 percent of African Americans said the activities of the Black Panther Party gave them pride, and 43 percent said the party represented their own views.[15] In fact, militant struggle had long been a part of black people's resistance to white supremacy. Mumia Abu-Jamal boldly documents this history in his 2004 book, *We Want Freedom*.

He writes, "The roots of armed resistance run deep in African American history. Only those who ignore this fact see the Black Panther Party as somehow foreign to our common historical inheritance."[16] In reality, the nonviolent segments cannot be distilled and separated from the revolutionary parts of the movement (though alienation and bad blood, encouraged by the state, often existed between them). Pacifist, middle-class black activists, including King, got much of their power from the specter of black resistance and the presence of armed black revolutionaries.[17]

In the spring of 1963, Martin Luther King Jr.'s Birmingham campaign was looking like it would be a repeat of the dismally failed action in Albany, Georgia (where a 9 month civil disobedience campaign in 1961 demonstrated the powerlessness of nonviolent protestors against a government with seemingly bottomless jails, and where, on July 24, 1962, rioting youth took over whole blocks for a night and forced the police to retreat from the ghetto, demonstrating that a year after the nonviolent campaign, black people in Albany still struggled against racism, but they had lost their preference for nonviolence). Then, on May 7 in Birmingham, after continued police violence, three thousand black people began fighting back, pelting the police with rocks and bottles. Just two days later, Birmingham—up until then an inflexible bastion of segregation—agreed to desegregate downtown stores, and President Kennedy backed the agreement with federal guarantees. The next day, after local white supremacists bombed a black home and a black business, thousands of black people rioted again, seizing a 9 block area, destroying police cars, injuring several cops (including the chief inspector), and burning white businesses. A month and a day later, President Kennedy was calling for Congress to pass the Civil Rights Act, ending several years of a strategy to stall the civil rights movement.[18] Perhaps the largest of the limited, if not hollow, victories of the civil rights movement came when black people demonstrated they would not remain peaceful forever.

Faced with the two alternatives, the white power structure chose to negotiate with the pacifists, and we have seen the results.

The claim that the US peace movement ended the war against Vietnam contains the usual set of flaws. The criticism has been well made by Ward Churchill and others,[19] so I'll only summarize it. With unforgivable self-righteousness, peace activists ignore that three to five million Indochinese died in the fight against the US military; tens of thousands of US troops were killed and hundreds of thousands wounded; other troops demoralized by all the bloodshed had become highly ineffective and rebellious;[20] and the US was losing political capital (and going fiscally bankrupt) to a point where pro-war politicians began calling for a strategic withdrawal (especially after the Tet Offensive proved the war to be "unwinnable," in the words of many at the time). The US government was not forced to pull out by peaceful protests; it was defeated politically and militarily. As evidence of this, Churchill cites the victory of Republican Richard Nixon, and the lack of even an anti-war nominee within the Democratic Party, in 1968, near the height of the anti-war movement. One could also add Nixon's reelection in 1972, after four years of escalation and genocide, to demonstrate the powerlessness of the peace movement in "speaking truth to power." In fact, the principled peace movement dissolved in tandem with the withdrawal of US troops (completed in 1973). The movement was less responsive to history's largest-ever bombing campaign, targeting civilians, which intensified after troop withdrawal, or the continued occupation of South Vietnam by a US-trained and -financed military dictatorship. In other words, the movement retired (and rewarded Nixon with reelection) once Americans, and not Vietnamese, were out of harm's way. The US peace movement failed to bring peace. US imperialism continued unabated, and though its chosen military strategy was defeated by the Vietnamese, the US still accomplished its overall policy objectives in due time, precisely because of the failure of the peace movement to make any domestic changes.

Some pacifists will point out the huge number of "conscientious objectors" who refused to fight, to salvage some semblance of a nonviolent victory. But it should be obvious that the proliferation of objectors and draft dodgers cannot redeem pacifist tactics. Especially in such a militaristic society, the likelihood of soldiers' refusing to fight is proportional to their expectations of facing a violent opposition that might kill or maim them. Without the violent resistance of the Vietnamese, there would have been no need for a draft; without a draft, the self-serving nonviolent resistance in North America would hardly have existed. Far more significant than passive conscientious objectors were the growing rebellions, especially by black, Latino, and indigenous troops, within the military. The US government's intentional plan, in response to black urban riots, of taking unemployed young black men off the streets and into the military, backfired.[21]

> Washington officials visiting Army bases were freaked out at the development of "Black militant" culture....Astonished brass would watch as local settler [white] officers would be forced to return salutes to New Afrikans [black soldiers] giving them the "Power" sign [raised fist]....Nixon had to get the troops out of Vietnam fast or risk losing his army.[22]

Fragging, sabotage, refusal to fight, rioting in the stockades, and aiding the enemy, all activities of US soldiers, contributed significantly to the US government's decision to pull out ground troops. As Colonel Robert D. Heinl stated in June 1971,

> By every conceivable indicator, our army that remains in Vietnam is in a state approaching collapse, with individual units avoiding or having refused combat, murdering their officers and non-commissioned officers, drug-ridden and dispirited where not near mutinous. Elsewhere than Vietnam the situation is nearly as serious.[23]

The Pentagon estimated that 3 percent of officers and noncoms killed in Vietnam from 1961 to 1972 were killed in fraggings by their own troops. This estimate doesn't even take into account killings by stabbing or shooting. In many instances, soldiers in a unit pooled their money to raise a bounty for the killing of an unpopular officer. Matthew Rinaldi identifies "working class blacks and Latinos" in the military, who did not identify with the "pacifism-at-any-price tactics" of the civil rights movement that had come before them, as major actors in the militant resistance that crippled the US military during the Vietnam War.[24]

And though they were less politically significant than resistance in the military in general, bombings and other acts of violence in protest of the war on white college campuses, including most of the elite universities, should not be ignored in favor of the pacifist whitewash. In the 1969–1970 school year (September through May), a conservative estimate counts 174 anti-war bombings on campuses and at least 70 off-campus bombings and other violent attacks targeting ROTC buildings, government buildings, and corporate offices. Additionally, 230 campus protests included physical violence, and 410 included damage to property.[25]

In conclusion, what was a very limited victory—the withdrawal of ground troops after many years of warfare—can be most clearly attributed to two factors: the successful and sustained violent resistance of the Vietnamese, which caused US policy-makers to realize they could not win; and the militant and often lethal resistance of the US ground troops themselves, which was caused by demoralization from the effective violence of their enemy and political militancy spreading from the contemporaneous black liberation movement. The domestic anti-war movement clearly worried US policy-makers,[26] but it had certainly not become powerful enough that we can say it "forced" the government to do anything, and, in any case, its most forceful elements used violent protests, bombings, and property destruction.

Perhaps confused by their own false history of the peace movement during the Vietnam War, US pacifist organizers in the 21st century seemed to expect a repeat of the victory that never happened in their plans to stop the invasion of Iraq. On February 15,

2003, as the US government moved toward war with Iraq, "week-end protests worldwide by millions of anti-war activists delivered a stinging rebuke to Washington and its allies....The unprecedented wave of demonstrations...further clouded US war plans," accord-ing to an article on the website of the nonviolent anti-war group United for Peace and Justice.[27] The article, which exults in the "mas-sive display of pacifist feeling," goes on to project that the "White House...appears to have been rattled by the surge in resistance to its calls for quick military action." The protests were the largest in history; excepting a few minor scuffles, they were entirely non-violent; and organizers extensively celebrated their massiveness and peacefulness. Some groups, like United for Peace and Justice, even suggested the protests might avert war. Of course, they were totally wrong, and the protests totally ineffective. The invasion occurred as planned, despite the millions of people nominally, peacefully, and powerlessly opposed to it. The anti-war movement did nothing to change the power relationships in the United States. Bush received substantial political capital for invading Iraq, and was not faced with a backlash until the war and occupation effort began to show signs of failure *due to the effective armed resistance of the Iraqi people.* The so-called opposition did not even manifest within the official political landscape. The one anti-war candidate in the Democratic Party,[28] Dennis Kucinich, was never for a moment taken seriously as a contender, and he and his supporters eventually fled their moral high ground to defer to the Democratic Party platform's support for the occupation of Iraq.

A good case study regarding the efficacy of nonviolent protest can be seen in Spain's involvement with the US-led occupation. Spain, with 1,300 troops, was one of the larger junior partners in the "Coalition of the Willing." More than *one million* Spaniards pro-tested the invasion, and 80 percent of the Spanish population was opposed to it,[29] but their commitment to peace ended there—they did nothing to actually prevent Spanish military support for the invasion and occupation. Because they remained passive and did nothing to disempower the leadership, they remained as powerless as the citizens of any democracy. Not only was Spanish prime minister Aznar able and allowed to go to war, he was expected by all forecasts to win reelection—until the bombings. On March 11, 2004, just days before the voting booths opened, multiple bombs planted by an Al-Qaida–linked cell exploded in Madrid train stations, killing 191 people and injuring thousands more. Directly because of this, Aznar and his party lost in the polls, and the Socialists, the major party with an anti-war platform, were elected into power.[30] The US-led coalition shrunk with the loss of 1,300 Spanish troops, and promptly shrunk again after the Dominican Republic and Honduras also pulled out their troops. Whereas millions of peaceful activists voting in the streets like good sheep have not weakened the brutal occupation in any measurable way, a few dozen terrorists willing to slaughter noncombatants were able to cause the withdrawal of more than a thousand occupation troops.

The actions and statements of cells affiliated with Al Qaida do not suggest that they want a meaningful peace in Iraq, nor do they demonstrate a concern for the well-being of the Iraqi people (a great many of whom they have blown to bits) so much as a concern for a particular vision of how Iraqi society should be organized, a vision that is extremely authoritarian, patriarchal, and fundamentalist. And, no doubt, what was possibly an easy decision to kill and maim hundreds of unarmed people, however strategically necessary such an action may have seemed, is connected to their authoritarianism and brutality, and most of all to the culture of intellectualism from which most terrorists come (although that is another topic entirely).

The morality of the situation becomes more complicated when compared to the massive US bombing campaign that intentionally killed hundreds of thousands of civilians in Germany and Japan during World War II. Whereas this campaign was much more brutal than the Madrid bombings, it is generally considered acceptable. The discrepancy that we may entertain between condemning the Madrid bombers (easy) and condemning the even more bloody-handed American pilots (not so easy, perhaps because among them we may find our own relatives—my grandfather, for example) should make us question whether our condemnation of terrorism really has anything to do with a respect for life. Because we are not fighting for an authoritarian world, or one in which blood is spilled in accordance with calculated rationales, the Madrid bombings do not present an example for action, but, rather, an important paradox. Do people who stick to peaceful tactics that have not proved effective in ending the war against Iraq really care more for human life than the Madrid terrorists? After all, many more than 191 Iraqi civilians have been killed for every 1,300 occupation troops stationed there. If anyone has to die (and the US invasion makes this tragedy inevitable), Spanish citizens bear more blame than Iraqis (just as German and Japanese citizens bore more blame than other victims of World War II). So far, no alternatives to terrorism have been developed within the relatively vulnerable belly of the beast to substantially weaken the occupation. Hence, the only real resistance is occurring in Iraq, where the US and its allies are most prepared to meet it, at great cost to the lives of guerrillas and noncombatants.

So much for the victories of pacifism.

It would also help to understand the extent of the idea's failures. A controversial but necessary example is that of the Holocaust.[31] For much of "the devouring," militant resistance was all but absent, so we can measure the efficacy of pacifist resistance alone. The Holocaust is also one of the few phenomena where victim-blaming is correctly seen as support or sympathy for the oppressor, so the occasional oppositional uprisings cannot be used to justify the repression and genocide, as happens elsewhere when pacifists blame authoritarian violence on the audacity of the oppressed to take militant direct action against that authority. Some pacifists have been so bold as to use examples of resistance to the Nazis, such as civil disobedience carried out by the Danes, to suggest that nonviolent resistance can work even in the worst conditions.[32] Is it really necessary to point out that the Danes, as Aryans faced a somewhat different set of consequences for resistance than the Nazis' primary victims? The Holocaust was only ended by the concerted, overwhelming violence of the Allied governments that destroyed the Nazi state (though, to be honest, they cared far more about redrawing the map of Europe than about saving the lives of Roma, Jews, gays, leftists, Soviet prisoners of war, and others; the Soviets tended to "purge" rescued prisoners of war, fearing that even if they were not guilty of desertion for surrendering, their contact with foreigners in the concentration camps had contaminated them ideologically).

The victims of the Holocaust, however, were not entirely passive. A large number of them took action to save lives and sabotage the Nazi death machine. Yehuda Bauer, who deals exclusively with Jewish victims of the Holocaust, emphatically documents this resistance. Up until 1942, "rabbis and other leaders...counseled against taking up arms," but they did not counsel passivity; rather, "resistance was nonviolent."[33] Clearly, it did not slow down the genocide or weaken the Nazis in any measurable way. Beginning in 1942, Jews began to resist violently, though there are still many examples of nonviolent resistance. In 1943, people in Denmark helped most of the country's seven thousand Jews escape to neutral Sweden. Similarly, in the same year, the government, Church, and people of Bulgaria stopped the deportation of Jews from that country.[34] In both of these cases, the rescued Jews were ultimately protected by military force and kept safe by the borders of a country not under direct German occupation at a time when the war was starting to look bleak for the Nazis. (Because of the violent onslaught of the Soviets, the Nazis temporarily overlooked the minor thwarting of their plans by Sweden and Bulgaria.) In 1941, the inhabitants of a ghetto in Vilnius, Lithuania, conducted a massive sit-down when the Nazis and local authorities prepared to deport them.[35] This act of civil disobedience may have delayed the deportation a short while, but it failed to save any lives.

PETER GELDERLOOS

A number of leaders of the Judenrat, the Jewish Councils established by the Nazis to govern the ghettos in compliance with
Nazi orders, accommodated the Nazis in an attempt not to rock
the boat, in the hope that as many Jews as possible would still be
alive at the end of the war. (This is an apt example because many
pacifists in the US today also believe that if you are rocking the
boat or causing conflict, you are doing something wrong.[36]) Bauer
writes, "In the end, the strategy failed, and those who had tried to
use it discovered with horror that they had become accomplices in
the Nazis' murder plan."[37] Other Jewish Council members were
bolder, and openly refused to cooperate with the Nazis. In Lvov,
Poland, the first council chairman refused to cooperate, and he
was duly killed and replaced. As Bauer points out, the replace-
ments were much more compliant (though even obedience didn't
save them, as they were all bound for the death camps; in the specific example of Lvov, the obedient replacement was killed anyway
just on suspicion of resistance). In Borszczow, Poland, the council
chairman refused to comply with Nazi orders, and he was shipped
off to the Belzec death camp.[38]

Other council members used a diversity of tactics, and they
were clearly more effective. In Kovno, Lithuania, they pretended
to comply with Nazi orders, but were secretly a part of the resistance. They successfully hid children about to be deported and
smuggled young men and women out of the ghetto so they could
fight with the partisans. In France, "both sections [of the council]
belonged to the underground and were in constant touch with
the resisters...and contributed significantly to the saving of most
of the Jews in the country."[39] Even where they did not personally
take part in violent resistance, they multiplied their effectiveness
immensely by supporting those who did.

And then there were the urban guerrillas and partisans who
fought violently against the Nazis. In April and May 1943, Jews
in the Warsaw ghetto rose up with smuggled, stolen, and homemade weapons. Seven hundred young men and women fought for

weeks, to the death, tying up thousands of Nazi troops and other resources needed on the collapsing Eastern Front. They knew they would be killed whether they were peaceful or not. By rebelling violently, they lived the last few weeks of their lives in freedom and resistance, and slowed down the Nazi war machine. Another armed rebellion broke out in the ghetto of Bialystok, Poland, on August 16, 1943, and continued for weeks.

Urban guerrillas such as a group composed of Jewish Zionists and Communists in Krakow, successfully blew up supply trains and railroads, sabotaged war factories, and assassinated government officials.[40] Jewish and other partisan groups throughout Poland, Czechoslovakia, Belarus, Ukraine, and the Baltic countries also carried out acts of sabotage on German supply lines and fought off SS troops. According to Bauer, "In eastern Poland, Lithuania, and the western Soviet Union, at least 15,000 Jewish partisans fought in the woods, and at least 5,000 unarmed Jews lived there, protected all or some of the time by the fighters."[41] In Poland, a group of partisans led by the Belsky brothers saved more than 1,200 Jewish men, women, and children, in part by carrying out revenge killings against those who captured or turned in fugitives. Similar partisan groups in France and Belgium sabotaged war infrastructure, assassinated Nazi officials, and helped people escape the death camps. A band of Jewish Communists in Belgium derailed a train that was taking people to Auschwitz, and helped several hundred of them to escape.[42] During a rebellion at the Sobibor death camps in October 1943, resisters killed several Nazi officers and allowed four hundred of the six hundred inmates to escape. Most of these were quickly killed, but about sixty survived to join the partisans. Two days after the revolt, Sobibor was closed down. A rebellion at Treblinka in August 1943 destroyed that death camp, and it was not rebuilt. Participants in another insurrection at Auschwitz in October 1944 destroyed one of the crematoria.[43] All of these violent uprisings slowed down the Holocaust. In comparison, nonviolent tactics (and, for that matter, the Allied governments whose bombers could easily have reached Auschwitz and other camps) failed to shut down or destroy a single extermination camp before the end of the war.

In the Holocaust, and less extreme examples from India to Birmingham, nonviolence failed to sufficiently empower its practitioners, whereas the use of a diversity of tactics got results. Put simply, if a movement is not a threat, it cannot change a system based on centralized coercion and violence,[44] and if that movement does not realize and exercise the power that makes it a threat, it cannot destroy such a system. In the world today, governments and corporations hold a near-total monopoly on power, a major aspect of which is violence. Unless we change the power relationships (and, preferably, destroy the infrastructure and culture of centralized power to make impossible the subjugation of the many to the few), those who currently benefit from the ubiquitous structural violence, who control the militaries, banks, bureaucracies, and corporations, will continue to call the shots. The elite cannot be persuaded by appeals to their conscience. Individuals who do change their minds and find a better morality will be fired, impeached, replaced, recalled, assassinated.

Time and again, people struggling not for some token reform but for complete liberation—the reclamation of control over our own lives and the power to negotiate our own relationships with the people and world around us—will find that nonviolence does not work, that we face a self-perpetuating power structure that is immune to appeals to conscience and strong enough to plow over the disobedient and uncooperative. We must reclaim histories of resistance to understand why we have failed in the past and how exactly we achieved the limited successes we did. We must also accept that all social struggles, except those carried out by a completely pacified and thus ineffective people, include a diversity of tactics. Realizing that nonviolence has never actually produced historical victories toward revolutionary goals opens the door to considering other serious faults of nonviolence.

2

NONVIOLENCE IS
R A C I S T

I do not mean to exchange insults, and I use the epithet *racist* only after careful consideration. Nonviolence is an inherently privileged position in the modern context. Besides the fact that the typical pacifist is quite clearly white and middle class, pacifism as an ideology comes from a privileged context. It ignores that violence is already here; that violence is an unavoidable, structurally integral part of the current social hierarchy; and that it is people of color who are most affected by that violence. Pacifism assumes that white people who grew up in the suburbs with all their basic needs met can counsel oppressed people, many of whom are people of color, to suffer patiently under an inconceivably greater violence, until such time as the Great White Father is swayed by the movement's demands or the pacifists achieve that legendary "critical mass."

People of color in the internal colonies of the US cannot defend themselves against police brutality or expropriate the means of survival to free themselves from economic servitude. They must wait for enough people of color who have attained more economic privilege (the "house slaves" of Malcolm X's analysis[1]) and conscientious white people to gather together and hold hands and sing songs. Then, they believe, change will surely come. People in Latin America must suffer patiently, like true martyrs, while white activists in the US "bear witness" and write to Congress. People in Iraq must not fight back. Only if they remain civilians will their deaths be counted and mourned by white peace activists who will, one of these days, muster a protest large enough to stop the war. Indigenous people need to wait just a little longer (say, another 500 years) under the shadow of genocide, slowly dying off on marginal lands, until—well, they're not a priority right now, so perhaps they need to organize a demonstration or two to win the attention and sympathy of the powerful. Or maybe they could go on strike, engage in Gandhian noncooperation? But wait—a majority of them are already unemployed, noncooperating, fully excluded from the functioning of the system.

Nonviolence declares that the American Indians could have fought off Columbus, George Washington, and all the other genocidal butchers with sit-ins; that Crazy Horse, by using violent resistance, became part of the cycle of violence, and was "as bad as" Custer. Nonviolence declares that Africans could have stopped the slave trade with hunger strikes and petitions, and that those who mutinied were as bad as their captors; that mutiny, a form of violence, led to more violence, and, thus, resistance led to more enslavement. Nonviolence refuses to recognize that it can only work for privileged people, who have a status protected by violence, as the perpetrators and beneficiaries of a violent hierarchy.

Pacifists must know, at least subconsciously, that nonviolence is an absurdly privileged position, so they make frequent usage of race by taking activists of color out of their contexts and selectively using them as spokespersons for nonviolence. Gandhi and Martin Luther King Jr. are turned into representatives for all people of color. Nelson Mandela was too, until it dawned on white pacifists that Mandela used nonviolence selectively, and that he actually was involved in liberation activities such as bombings and preparation for armed uprising.[2] Even Gandhi and King agreed it was necessary to support armed liberation movements (citing as examples those in Palestine and Vietnam, respectively) where there was no nonviolent alternative, clearly prioritizing goals over particular tactics. But the mostly white pacifists of today erase this part of the history and re-create nonviolence to fit their comfort level, even while "claiming the mantle" of Martin Luther King Jr. and Gandhi.[3] One gets the impression that if Martin Luther King

Jr. were to come in disguise to one of these pacifist vigils, he would not be allowed to speak. As he pointed out:

> Apart from bigots and backlashers, it seems to be a malady even among those whites who like to regard themselves as "enlightened." I would especially refer to those who counsel, "Wait!" and to those who say that they sympathize with our goals but cannot condone our methods of direct-action in pursuit of those goals. I wonder at men who dare to feel that they have some paternalistic right to set the timetable for another man's liberation.
>
> Over the past several years, I must say, I have been gravely disappointed with such white "moderates." I am often inclined to think that they are more of a stumbling block to the Negro's progress than the White Citizen's Counciler [sic] or the Ku Klux Klanner.[4]

And it must be added that privileged white people were instrumental in appointing activists such as Gandhi and King to positions of leadership on a national scale. Among white activists and, not coincidentally, the white-supremacist ruling class, the civil rights–era March on Washington is associated first and foremost with Martin Luther King Jr.'s "I Have a Dream" speech. Mostly absent from the white consciousness, but at least as influential to black people, was Malcolm X's perspective, as articulated in his speech criticizing the march's leadership.

> It was the grassroots out there in the street. It scared the white man to death, scared the white power structure in Washington, DC, to death; I was there. When they found out this black steamroller was going to come down on the capital, they called in...these national Negro leaders that you respect and told them, "Call it off." Kennedy said, "Look, you all are letting this thing go too far." And Old Tom said, "Boss, I can't stop it because I didn't start it." I'm telling you what they said. They said, "I'm not even in it, much less at the head of it." They said, "These Negroes are doing things on their

own. They're running ahead of us." And that old shrewd fox, he said, "If you all aren't in it, I'll put you in it. I'll put you at the head of it. I'll endorse it. I'll welcome it....

This is what they did at the march on Washington. They joined it...became part of it, took it over. And as they took it over, it lost its militancy. It ceased to be angry, it ceased to be hot, it ceased to be uncompromising. Why, it even ceased to be a march. It became a picnic, a circus. Nothing but a circus, with clowns and all....

No, it was a sellout. It was a takeover....They controlled it so tight, they told those Negroes what time to hit town, where to stop, what signs to carry, what song to sing, what speech they could make, and what speech they couldn't make, and then told them to get out of town by sundown.[5]

The end result of the march was to invest significant movement resources, at a critical time, in an ultimately pacifying event. In the words of Bayard Rustin, one of the chief organizers of the march, "You start to organize a mass march by making an ugly assumption. You assume that everyone who is coming has the mentality of a three-year-old."[6] Demonstrators received premade protest signs with government-approved slogans; the speeches of several protest leaders, including SNCC chairman John Lewis, were censored to take out threats of armed struggle and criticisms of the government's civil rights bill; and, just as Malcolm X described, at the end, the whole crowd was told to leave as soon as possible.

Though he enjoys comparatively little attention in mainstream histories, Malcolm X was extremely influential on the black liberation movement, and he was recognized as such by the movement itself and by government forces charged with destroying the movement. In an internal memo, the FBI addresses the need to prevent the rise of a black "messiah" as part of its Counter Intelligence Program. According to the FBI, it is Malcolm X who "might have been such a 'messiah;' he is the martyr of the movement today."[7] The fact that Malcolm X was singled out by the FBI as a major threat raises the possibility of state involvement with his assassination;[8] certainly other nonpacifist black activists, who were identified by the FBI as particularly effective organizers, were targeted for elimination by means including assassination.[9] Meanwhile, Martin Luther King Jr. was allowed his celebrity and influence until he became more radical, spoke of anti-capitalist revolution, and advocated solidarity with the armed struggle of the Vietnamese.

In effect, white activists, particularly those interested in minimizing the role of militant and armed struggle, assist the state in assassinating Malcolm X (and similar revolutionaries). They perform the cleaner half of the job, in disappearing his memory and erasing him from history.[10] And despite their absurdly disproportionate professions of devotion to him (there were, after all, a few other people who took part in the civil rights movement), they similarly help assassinate Martin Luther King Jr., though in his case a more Orwellian method (assassinate, reformulate, and co-opt) is used. Darren Parker, a black activist and consultant to grassroots groups whose criticisms have contributed to my own understanding of nonviolence, writes,

> The number of times people quote King is one of the most off-putting things for most black folk because they know how much his life was focused on the race struggle…and when you actually read King, you tend to wonder why the parts critical of white people, which are the majority of the things he said and wrote, never get quoted.[11]

Thus King's more disturbing (to white people) criticism of racism is avoided,[12] and his clichéd prescriptions for feel-good, nonviolent activism are repeated ad nauseum, allowing white pacifists to cash in on an authoritative cultural resource to confirm their nonviolent activism and prevent the acknowledgement of the racism inherent in their position by associating themselves with a noncontroversial black figurehead.

Pacifists' revising of history to remove examples of militant struggles against white supremacy cannot be divorced from a racism that is inherent in the pacifist position. It is impossible to claim support for, much less solidarity with, people of color in their struggles when unavoidably significant groups such as the Black Panther Party, the American Indian Movement, the Brown Berets, and the Vietcong are actively ignored in favor of a homogeneous picture of anti-racist struggle that acknowledges only those segments that do not contradict the relatively comfortable vision of revolution preferred mostly by white radicals. Claims of support and solidarity become even more pretentious when white pacifists draft rules of acceptable tactics and impose them across the movement, in denial of the importance of race, class background, and other contextual factors.

The point is not that white activists, in order to be anti-racist, need to uncritically support any Asian, Latino, indigenous, or black resistance group that pops up. However, there is a Eurocentric universalism in the idea that we are all part of the same homogeneous struggle and white people at the heart of the Empire can tell people of color and people in the (neo)colonies the best way to resist. The people most affected by a system of oppression should be at the forefront of the struggle against that particular oppression,[13] yet pacifism again and again produces organizations and movements of white people illuminating the path and leading the way to save brown people, because the imperative of nonviolence overrides the basic respect of trusting people to liberate themselves. Whenever white pacifists concern themselves with a cause that affects people of color, and resisters among the affected people of color do not conform to the particular definition of nonviolence in use, the white activists place themselves as the teachers and guides, creating a dynamic that is remarkably colonial. Of course, this is largely a function of whiteness (a socially constructed worldview taught diffusively to all people identified by society as "white"). Militant white activists can and do incur similar problems when

they disrespect allies of color by dictating the appropriate, ortho-
dox method of struggle.

The Weather Underground and other militant white groups
of the 1960s and 70s did a horrible job of extending solidarity
to the black liberation movement, voicing support but withhold-
ing any material aid, in part because they viewed themselves as a
vanguard and the black groups as ideological competitors. Other
white organizations, such as the Liberation Support Movement,
used their support to exercise control over the anti-colonial liberation movements they claimed to be acting in solidarity with,[14]
much the way a government aid agency operates.

Interestingly, even among militant white activists, racism encourages passivity. One of the problems of the Weather Underground
is that they were claiming to fight alongside black and Vietnamese people, but this was just posturing—they conducted
harmless, symbolic bombings and disdained actions likely to
put their own lives at risk. Today, their veterans are not dead
or imprisoned (excepting three victims of an early explosives-
making accident and those who left Weather to fight alongside members of the Black Liberation Army); they are living
comfortably as academics and professionals.[15] Militant white
anarchists in North America today exhibit similar tendencies.
Many of the most vocal disdain ongoing liberation struggles,
denouncing them as "not anarchist," rather than supporting
their most anti-authoritarian elements. The result is that these
hard-core (and, at the same time, armchair) anarchists can find
no real (and dangerous) resistance worthy of their support, so
they stick to militant postures and the violence of ideological
hairsplitting.

A white supremacist system punishes the resistance of people
of color more harshly than the resistance of white people. Even
white activists who have made ourselves aware of the dynamics
of racism find the resulting privilege, one of socially guaranteed
safety, difficult to relinquish. Accordingly, those who challenge

white supremacy directly and militantly will seem threatening to us. Mumia Abu-Jamal writes:

> The accolades and bouquets of late-20th-century Black struggle were awarded to veterans of the civil rights struggle epitomized by the martyred Rev. Dr. Martin Luther King Jr. Elevated by white and Black elites to the heights of social acceptance, Dr. King's message of Christian forbearance and his turn-the-other-cheek doctrine were calming to the white psyche. To Americans bred for comfort, Dr. King was, above all, safe.

> The Black Panther Party was the antithesis of Dr. King.

> The Party was not a civil rights group...but practiced the human right of self-defense....The Black Panther Party made (white) Americans feel many things, but safe wasn't one of them.[16]

White pacifists (and even bourgeois black pacifists) are afraid of the total abolition of the white supremacist, capitalist system. They preach nonviolence to the people at the bottom of the racial and economic hierarchy precisely because nonviolence is ineffective, and any revolution launched 'by those people," provided it remains nonviolent, will be unable to fully unseat white people and rich people from their privileged positions. Even strains of nonviolence that seek to abolish the state aim to do so by transforming it (and converting the people in power); thus, nonviolence requires that activists attempt to influence the power structure, which requires that they approach it, which means that privileged people, who have better access to power, will retain control of any movement as the gatekeepers and intermediaries who allow the masses to "speak truth to power."

In November 2003, School of the Americas Watch (SOAW) activists organized an anti-oppression discussion during their annual pacifist vigil outside Fort Benning Army Base (which houses the School of the Americas, a military-training school prominently connected to human-rights abuses in Latin America). The orga-nizers of the discussion had a difficult time getting the white, middle-class participants (by far the dominant demographic at the explicitly nonviolent vigil) to focus on oppressive dynamics (such as racism, classism, sexism, and transphobia) within the organiza-tion and among activists associated with SOAW's anti-militarist efforts. Instead, people at the discussion, particularly older, white, self-proclaimed pacifists, kept returning to forms of oppression practiced by some external force—the police keeping an eye on the vigil, or the military subjugating people in Latin America. It was quite apparent that self-criticism (and -improvement) was an unde-sirable option; the preferable alternative was to focus on the faults of a violent other, emphasizing their own victimization by (and, hence, moral superiority to) the forces of state power. Eventually, a number of veteran activists of color who attended the discussion were able to move attention to the many forms of racism within the anti-SOA milieu that prevented it from attracting more sup-port from nonprivileged populations. Perhaps their major criti-cism, in pointing out the racism they witnessed, was against the organization's practice of pacifism. They spoke against the white pacifists' privileged, comfortable take on activism, and lambasted the casual, entertaining, celebratory attitude of the protest, with its pretensions of being revolutionary, even of being a protest.

One black woman was particularly incensed at an experience she had had while taking a bus down to the Fort Benning vigil with other anti-SOA activists. During a conversation with a white activist, she stated that she did not support the practice of non-violence. That activist then told her she was "on the wrong bus" and did not belong at the protest. When I related this story and the other criticisms made by people of color during the discus-sion to a listserv of SOAW-affiliated former prisoners (after serv-ing a fully voluntary, six-month-maximum prison sentence, they gave themselves the honorific title "prisoner of conscience"), one white peace activist wrote back to me that she was surprised that a black woman would be ideologically opposed to nonviolence, in spite of Martin Luther King Jr. and the legacy of the civil rights movement.[17]

Beneath their frequent and manipulative usage of people of color as figureheads and tame spokespersons, pacifists follow a tactical and ideological framework formulated almost exclusively by white theorists. Whereas revolutionary activists are hard-pressed to find white theorists with anything relevant to say regarding the methods of militant struggle, the teachers of pacifism are primarily white (for example; David Dellinger, the Berrigans, George Lakey, Gene Sharp, Dorothy Day, and AJ Muste). An article espousing nonviolence published, appropriately enough, in *The Nation*, drops Gandhi's name like a banner but primarily quotes white activists and scholars to articulate a more precise strategy.[18] Another article on nonviolence, recommended by a pacifist anti-SOA activist to nonpacifist activists who doubted pacifism's strategic depth, relies solely on white sources.[19] A book popular among US pacifists states that "America has more often been the teacher than the student of the nonviolent ideal."[20]

Pacifists would also do well to examine the color of violence. When we mention riots, whom do we envision? White activists committing property destruction as a form of civil disobedience may stretch, but do not usually lose, the protective covering of "nonviolence." People of color engaged in politically motivated property destruction, unless strictly within the rubric of a white activist–organized protest, are banished to the realm of violence, denied consideration as activists, not portrayed as conscientious.

The racism of the judicial system, a major and violent component of our society, though one rarely prioritized for opposition by pacifists, has had a major impact on the American psyche. Violence and criminality are nearly interchangeable concepts (consider how comfortable pacifists are in using the terminology of statist morality—for example, "justice"—as their own), and a chief purpose of both concepts is to establish blame. Just as criminals deserve repression and punishment, people who use violence deserve the inevitable karmic violent consequences; this is integral to the pacifist position. They may deny believing that anyone deserves to have violence used against them, but a stock argument common among pacifists is that revolutionaries should not use violence because the state will then use this to "justify" violent repression. Well, to whom is this violent repression justified, and why aren't those who claim to be against violence trying to un-justify it? Why do nonviolent activists seek to change society's morality in how it views oppression or war, but accept the morality of repression as natural and untouchable?

This idea of the inevitable repressive consequences of militancy frequently goes beyond hypocrisy to outright victim-blaming and approval of repressive violence. People of color who are oppressed with police and structural violence every day are counseled against responding with violence because that would justify the state violence already mobilized against them. Victim-blaming was a key part of pacifist discourse, strategy even, in the 1960s and 70s, when many white activists helped justify state actions and neutralize what could have become anti-government outrage at violent state repression of black and other liberation movements, such as the police assassinations of Panther organizers Fred Hampton and Mark Clark. Rather than supporting and aiding the Panthers, white pacifists found it more fashionable to state that they had "provoked violence" and "brought this on themselves."[21]

More recently, at the previously mentioned anarchist conference, I charged that the US anti-war movement deserved to share the blame in the deaths of three million Vietnamese for being so accommodating to state power. A pacifist, anarchist, and Christian Peacemaker responded to my charge by stating that the blame belonged with (I expected him to say the US military alone, but no!) Ho Chi Minh and the Vietnamese leadership for practicing armed struggle.[22] (Either this pacifist considers the Vietnamese people unable to have made the highly popular step toward violent resistance themselves, or he blames them as well.) One gets the impression that if more Gypsies, Jews, gays, and others had violently resisted the Holocaust, pacifists would find it convenient to blame that little phenomenon on the absence of an exclusively pacifist opposition as well.

By preaching nonviolence, and abandoning to state repression those who do not listen obediently, white activists who think they are concerned about racism are actually enacting a paternalistic relationship and fulfilling the useful role of pacifying the oppressed. The pacification, through nonviolence, of people of color intersects with the preference of white supremacist power structures to disarm the oppressed. The celebrated civil rights leaders, including King, were instrumental to the government's "bullet and ballot" strategy in isolating and destroying militant black activists and manipulating the remainder to support a weakened, pro-government agenda centered around voter registration. In fact, the NAACP and the Southern Christian Leadership Council (SCLC) got paid by the government for their services.[23] (And the Student Non-Violent Coordinating Committee (SNCC) was largely dependent on the donations of wealthy liberal benefactors, which it lost when it adopted a more militant stance, a factor that contributed to its collapse.)[24]

A century earlier, one of the major activities of the Ku Klux Klan in the years following the Civil War was to disarm the entire black population of the South, stealing any weapons they could find from newly "freed" black people, often with the assistance of the police. In fact, the Klan acted largely as a paramilitary force for the state in times of unrest, and both the Klan and modern US police forces have roots in the antebellum slave patrols, which regularly terrorized black people as a form of control, in what might be described as the original policy of racial profiling.[25] Today, with the security of the racial hierarchy assured, the Klan has fallen into the background, the police retain their weapons, and pacifists who think themselves allies urge black people not to re-arm themselves, ostracizing those who do.

A generation after the failure of the civil rights movement, black resistance gave birth to hip-hop, which mainstream cultural forces such as the recording industry, clothing manufacturers, and for-profit media (that is, white-owned businesses) capitalize and purchase. These capitalist cultural forces, which have been protected by the disarming of black people and enriched by their evolving slavery, wax pacifist and decry the prevalence of lyrics about shooting (back at) cops. Hip-hop artists bonded to the major record labels largely abandon the glorification of anti-state violence and replace it with an increase in the more fashionable violence against women. The appearance of nonviolence, in the case of black people not arming themselves or advocating struggle against police, is, in fact, a reflection of the triumph of a previous violence.

The massive interpersonal violence of the Klan created a material shift that is maintained by systematized and less visible police violence. At the same time, the cultural power of white elites, itself gained and preserved through all sorts of economic and government violence, is used to co-opt black culture to foster a celebration of some of the same ideological constructs that justified kidnapping, enslaving, and lynching black people in the first place, while channeling the anger from generations of abuse into cycles of violence within black communities, rather than allowing it to foment violence against the all-too-deserving authorities. In the power dynamic described in this brief historical sketch, and in so many other histories of racial oppression, people who insist on nonviolence among the oppressed, if they are to have any role, end up doing the work of the white supremacist power structure whether they mean to or not.

Robert Williams provided an alternative to this legacy of disarmament. Sadly, his story is left out of the dominant narrative found in state-sanctioned school textbooks, and, if proponents of nonviolence have anything to say about it, is also excluded from the movement's self-narrative and understanding of its own history. Beginning in 1957, Robert Williams armed the NAACP chapter in Monroe, North Carolina, to repel attacks from the Ku Klux Klan and the police. Williams influenced the formation of other armed self-defense groups, including the Deacons for Defense and Justice, which grew to include fifty chapters throughout the South that protected black communities and civil rights workers.[26] It is exactly these stories of empowerment that white pacifists ignore or blot out.

Nonviolence in the hands of white people has been and continues to be a colonial enterprise. White elites instruct the natives in how to run their economies and governments, while white dissidents instruct the natives in how to run their resistance. On April 20, 2006, a co-founder of Food Not Bombs (FNB), the majority-white anti-authoritarian group which serves free food in public places through one hundred chapters (mostly in North America, Australia, and Europe), sent out a call for support for the new FNB chapter in Nigeria.

> This March Food Not Bombs co-founder Keith McHenry and local Nigerian volunteer Yinka Dada visited the people suffering in the shadow of Nigeria's oil refineries. While conditions in the region are terrible, bombs are not a good way to improve conditions. The crisis in Nigeria has contributed to oil prices hitting a record $72 a barrel. It's understandable that people are frustrated that the profits of their resources are enriching foreign companies while their environment is polluted and they live in poverty. Food Not Bombs is offering a nonviolent solution.[27]

The Food Not Bombs call for support condemned the actions of the rebel militia, MEND, which is seeking autonomy for the Ijaw people of the Niger Delta and an end to the destructive oil industry (whereas FNB "welcomed Nigerian President Olusegun Obasanjo's announcement of new jobs in the Delta Region" from oil revenues). MEND had kidnapped several foreign (US and European) oil-company employees to demand an end to government repression and corporate exploitation (the hostages were released unharmed). Curiously, while they condemned the kidnapping, Food *Not Bombs* failed to mention the *bombing,* by the Nigerian military under President Obasanjo, of several Ijaw villages believed to support MEND. And while there is no evidence that the "nonviolent solution" they say they are "offering" will do anything to free Nigerians from the exploitation and oppression they suffer, if nonviolence were implemented among Nigerians that would surely avert the government's "crisis" and bring oil prices back down, which, I suppose, makes things more peaceful in North America.

Faced with the total repression of the white supremacist system, the obvious uselessness of the political process, and the shameless efforts of a dissident elite to exploit and control the rage of the oppressed, it should be no surprise or controversy at all that "the colonized man finds his freedom in and through violence," to use the words of Frantz Fanon, the doctor from Martinique who authored one of the most important works on the struggle against colonialism.[28] Most white people have enough privilege and latitude that we may mistake these generously long, velvet-padded chains for freedom, so we comfortably agitate within the parameters of democratic society (the borders of which are composed of violently enforced racial, economic, sexual, and governmental structures). Some of us are further mistaken in assuming that all people face these same circumstances, and expect people of color to exercise privileges they don't actually have. But beyond the strategic necessity of attacking the state with all means available to us, have those of us not faced with daily police intimidation, degradation, and subordination considered the uplifting effect of forcefully fighting back? Frantz Fanon writes, about the psychology of colonialism and of violence in pursuit of liberation, "At the level of individuals, violence [as a part of liberation struggle] is a cleansing force. It frees the native from his inferiority complex and from his despair and inaction; it makes him fearless and restores his self-respect."[29]

But proponents of nonviolence who come from privileged backgrounds, with material and psychological comforts guaranteed and protected by a violent order, do not grow up with an inferiority complex violently pounded into them. The arrogance of pacifists' assumption that they can dictate which forms of struggle are moral and effective to people who live in far different, far more violent circumstances is astounding. Suburban white people who lecture children of the Jenin refugee camp or the Colombian killing fields on resistance bear a striking similarity to, say, World Bank economists who dictate "good" agricultural practices to Indian farmers who have inherited centuries-old agricultural traditions. And the benign relationship of privileged people to global systems of violence should raise serious questions as to the sincerity of privileged people, in this case white people, who espouse nonviolence. To quote Darren Parker again, "The appearance, at least, of a nonviolent spirit is much easier to attain when one is not the direct recipient of the injustice and may in fact simply represent psychological distance. After all, it's much easier to 'Love thy enemy' when they are not actually your enemy."[30]

Yes, people of color, poor people, and people from the Global South have advocated nonviolence (though typically such pacifists come from more privileged strata of their communities); however, only through a highly active sense of superiority can white activists judge and condemn oppressed people who do not do so. True, regardless of privilege, we should be able to trust our own analysis, but when that analysis rests on a dubious moral high ground and a conveniently selective interpretation of what constitutes violence, chances are our self-criticism has fallen asleep on the job. When we understand that privileged people derive material benefits from the exploitation of oppressed people, and that this means we benefit from the violence used to keep them down, we cannot sincerely condemn them for violently rebelling against the structural violence that privileges us. (Those who have ever condemned the violent resistance of people who have grown up in more oppressive circumstances than themselves should think about this the next time they eat a banana or drink a cup of coffee.)

I hope it is well understood that the government uses more violent forms of repression against people of color in resistance than against white people. When Oglala traditionals and the American Indian Movement stood up on Pine Ridge Reservation in the 1970s to assert a little independence and to organize against the endemic bullying of the imposed "tribal government," the Pentagon, FBI, US Marshals, and Bureau of Indian Affairs instituted a full-fledged counterinsurgency program that resulted in daily violence and dozens of deaths. According to Ward Churchill and Jim Vander Wall, "The principle of armed self-defense had, for the dissidents, become a necessity of survival."[31]

The only proponents of nonviolence I have ever heard reject even the legitimacy of self-defense have been white, and though they may hold up their Oscar Romeros, they and their families have not personally had their survival threatened as a result of their activism.[32] I have a hard time believing that their aversion to violence has as much to do with principles as with privilege and ignorance. And beyond mere self-defense, whether individuals have faced the possibility of having to fight back to survive or to improve their lives depends largely on the color of their skin and their place in various national and global hierarchies of oppression. It is these experiences that nonviolence ignores by treating violence as a moral issue or a chosen thing.

The culturally sensitive alternative within pacifism is that privileged activists allow, or even support, militant resistance in the Global South, and possibly in the internal colonies of the Euro/American states, and only advocate nonviolence to people with a similarly privileged background. This formulation presents a new racism, suggesting that the fighting and dying be carried out by people of color in the more overtly oppressive states of the Global South, while privileged citizens of the imperial centers may be contented with more contextually appropriate forms of resistance such as protest rallies and sit-ins.

An anti-racist analysis, on the other hand, requires white people to recognize that the violence against which people of color must defend themselves originates in the white "First World." Thus, appropriate resistance to a regime that wages war against colonized people across the globe is to bring the war home; to build an anti-authoritarian, cooperative, and anti-racist culture among white people; to attack institutions of imperialism; and to extend support to oppressed people in resistance without under-mining the sovereignty of their struggle. However, nonabsolutist pacifists who allow for a little cultural relativism are typically less likely to support armed revolution when the fighting gets close to home. The thinking is that Palestinians, for example, may engage in militant struggle because they live under a violent regime, but for the brutalized residents of the nearest urban ghetto to form guerrilla units would be "inappropriate" or "irresponsible." This is the "not in my backyard" tendency, which is fueled by the recogni-tion that a revolution *there* would be exciting, but a revolution *here* would deprive privileged activists of our comfort. Also present is the latent fear of racial uprising, which is assuaged only when it is subordinated to a nonviolent ethic. Black people marching is pho-togenic. Black people with guns evokes the violent crime reports on the nightly news. American Indians holding a press conference is laudable. American Indians ready, willing, and able to take their land back is a trifle disturbing. Thus, white peoples' support for, and familiarity with, revolutionaries of color on the home front is limited to inert martyrs—the dead and the imprisoned.

The contradiction in ostensibly revolutionary pacifism is that revolution is never safe, but to the vast majority of its practitioners and advocates, pacifism is about staying safe, not getting hurt, not alienating anyone, not giving anyone a bitter pill to swallow. In making the connection between pacifism and the self-preservation of privileged activists, Ward Churchill quotes a pacifist organizer during the Vietnam era who denounced the revolutionary tactics of the Black Panther Party and Weather Underground because those tactics were "a really dangerous thing for all of us...they run the very real risk of bringing the same sort of violent repression [as seen in the police assassination of Fred Hampton] down on all of us."[33] Or, to quote David Gilbert, who is serving an effective life sentence for his actions as a member of the Weather Underground who went on to support the Black Liberation Army, "Whites had something to protect. It was comfortable to be at the peak of a morally prestigious movement for change while Black people were taking the main casualties for the struggle."[34]

The pacifist desire for safety continues today. In 2003, a non-violent activist reassured a Seattle newspaper about the character of planned protests. "I'm not saying that we would not support civil disobedience," Woldt said. "That has been part of the peace movement that church people have engaged in, but we are not into property damage or anything that creates negative consequences for us."[35]

And on a listserv for a radical environmental campaign in 2004, a law student and activist, after inviting an open discussion of tactics, advocated an end to the mention of nonpacifist tactics and demanded a strict adherence to nonviolence on the grounds that nonpacifist groups "get annihilated."[36] Another activist (and, incidentally, one of the other law students on the list) agreed, adding, "I think that having a discussion about violent tactics on this list is playing with fire, and it is putting everyone at risk." She was also concerned that "two of us will be facing the star chamber of the ethics committee of the Bar Association sometime in the near future."[37]

Of course, proponents of militancy must understand that there is a great need for caution when we discuss tactics, especially via e-mail, and that we face the hurdle of building support for actions that are more likely to get us harassed or imprisoned, even if all we do is discuss them. However, in this example, the two law students were not saying that the group should discuss only legal tactics or hypothetical tactics, they were saying that the group should discuss only nonviolent tactics. Since it had been billed as a discussion to help the group create ideological common ground, this was a manipulative way of using threats of government repression to prevent the group from even considering anything other than an explicitly nonviolent philosophy.

Because of the weighty self-interest of white people in preventing revolutionary uprisings in their own backyard, there has been a long history of betrayal by white pacifists who have condemned and abandoned revolutionary groups to state violence. Rather than "putting themselves in harm's way" to protect members of the black, brown, and red liberation movements (a protection their privilege might have adequately conferred because of how costly it would have been for the government to murder affluent white people in the midst of all the dissension spurred by heavy losses in Vietnam), conscientious pacifists ignored the brutalization, imprisonment, and assassination of Black Panthers, American Indian Movement activists, and others. Worse still, they encouraged the state repression and claimed that the revolutionaries deserved it by engaging in militant resistance. (Nowadays, they are claiming that the liberationists' ultimate defeat, which pacifists facilitated, is proof of the ineffectiveness of liberationists' tactics.) Revered pacifist David Dellinger admits that "one of the factors that induces serious revolutionaries and discouraged ghetto-dwellers to conclude that nonviolence is incapable of being developed into a method adequate to their needs is this very tendency of pacifists to line up, in moments of conflict, with the status quo."[38] David Gilbert concludes that "failure to develop solidarity with the Black and other liberation struggles within the US (Native American, Chicano/Mexican, Puerto Rican) is one of the several factors that caused our movement to fall apart in the mid-70s."[39] Mumia Abu-Jamal questions, were white radicals "really ready to embark on a revolution, one that did not prize whiteness?"[40]

At first, nonviolence seems like a clear moral position that has little to do with race. This view is based on the simplistic assumption that violence is first and foremost something that we choose. But which people in this world have the privilege to choose violence, and which people live in violent circumstances whether they want to or not? Generally, nonviolence is a privileged practice, one that comes out of the experiences of white people, and it does not always make sense for people without white privilege or for white people attempting to destroy the system of privilege and oppression.

Many people of color have also used nonviolence, which in certain circumstances has been an effective way to stay safe in the face of violent discrimination, while seeking limited reforms that do not ultimately change the distribution of power in society. The use of nonviolence by people of color has generally been a compromise to a white power structure. Recognizing that the white power structure prefers the oppressed to be nonviolent, some people have chosen to use nonviolent tactics to forestall extreme repression, massacres, or even genocide. Movements of people of color peacefully pursuing revolutionary goals have tended to use a form of nonviolence that is less absolute, and more confrontational and dangerous, than the kind of nonviolence preserved in North America today. And even then, the practice of nonviolence is often subsidized by whites in power,[41] used by white dissidents or government officials to manipulate the movement for their comfort, and usually abandoned by large portions of the grassroots in favor of more militant tactics. The use of nonviolence to preserve white privilege, within the movement or society at large, is still common today.

On inspection, nonviolence proves to be tangled up with dynamics of race and power. Race is essential to our experience of oppression and of resistance. A long standing component of racism has been the assumption that Europeans, or European settlers on other continents, have known what is best for people they considered "less civilized." People fighting against racism must unmistakably end this tradition and recognize that the imperative for each community to be able to determine its own form of resistance based on its own experiences leaves any priority given to pacifism in the dust. Furthermore, the fact that much of the violence faced by people of color around the world originates in the power structure that privileges white people should lend white people greater urgency in pushing the boundaries for the level of militancy that is considered acceptable in white communities. In other words, for those of us who are white, it becomes our duty to build our own militant culture of resistance, and, contrary to the role of teacher historically self-appointed to white people, we have a great deal to learn from the struggles of people of color. White radicals must educate other white people about why people of color are justified in rebelling violently and why we too should use a diversity of tactics to free ourselves, struggle in solidarity with all who have rejected their place as the lackeys or slaves of the elite, and end these global systems of oppression and exploitation.

3

NONVIOLENCE IS STATIST

Put quite plainly, nonviolence ensures a state monopoly on violence. States—the centralized bureaucracies that protect capitalism; preserve a white supremacist, patriarchal order; and implement imperialist expansion—survive by assuming the role of the sole legitimate purveyor of violent force within their territory. Any struggle against oppression necessitates a conflict with the state. Pacifists do the state's work by pacifying the opposition in advance.[1] States, for their part, discourage militancy within the opposition, and encourage passivity.

Some pacifists obscure this mutual relationship by claiming that the government would just love to see them abandon their nonviolent discipline and give in to violence, that the government even encourages violence from dissidents, and that many activists urging militancy are, in fact, government provocateurs.[2] Thus, they argue, it is the militant activists who are playing into the hands of the state. Although in some instances the US government has used infiltrators to encourage resistance groups to hoard weapons or plan violent actions (for example, in the cases of the Molly Maguires and Jonathan Jackson's attempted courthouse strike[3]), a critical distinction must be made. The government only encourages violence when it is sure that the violence can be contained and will not get out of hand. In the end, causing a militant resistance group to act prematurely or walk into a trap eliminates the group's potential for violence by guaranteeing an easy life sentence or allowing authorities to sidestep the judicial process and kill off the radicals more quickly. On the whole, and in nearly all other instances, the authorities pacify the population and discourage violent rebellion.

There is a clear reason for this. Contrary to the fatuous claims of pacifists that they somehow empower themselves by cutting out the greater part of their tactical options, governments everywhere recognize that unconstrained revolutionary activism poses the greater threat of changing the distribution of power in society. Though the state always reserves the right to repress whomever it wishes, modern "democratic" governments treat nonviolent social movements with revolutionary goals as potential, rather than actual, threats. They spy on such movements to stay aware of developments, and they use a carrot-and-stick approach to herd such movements into fully peaceful, legal, and ineffective channels. Nonviolent groups may be subjected to beatings, but such groups are not targeted for elimination (except by regressive governments or governments facing a period of emergency that threatens their stability).

On the other hand, the state treats militant groups (those same groups pacifists deem ineffective) as actual threats and attempts to neutralize them with highly developed counterinsurgency and domestic warfare operations. Hundreds of union organizers, anarchists, communists, and militant farmers were killed in the anti-capitalist struggles of the late 19th and early 20th centuries. During the last generation's liberation struggles, FBI-supported paramilitaries killed sixty American Indian Movement (AIM) activists and supporters on the Pine Ridge Reservation alone, and the FBI, local police, and paid agents killed dozens of members of the Black Panther Party, Republic of New Afrika, the Black Liberation Army, and other groups.[4]

Vast resources were mobilized toward infiltrating and destroying militant revolutionary organizations during the COINTELPRO era. Any hint of militant organizing by colonized indigenous peoples, Puerto Ricans, and others within US territorial purview still incurs violent repression. Prior to September 11, the FBI had named the saboteurs and arsonists of the Earth Liberation Front (ELF) and Animal Liberation Front (ALF) as the greatest domestic terrorism threats, even though these two groups had killed exactly zero people. Even since the bombings of the World Trade Center and the Pentagon, the ELF and ALF have remained priorities for government repression, as seen in the arrests of over a dozen alleged ELF/ALF members; the agreement of many of these prisoners to become snitches after one of them died in a suspicious suicide and all of them had been threatened with life sentences; and the incarceration of several members of an above-ground animal rights group for hounding a vivisection company with an aggressive boycott—which the government has termed "animal enterprise terrorism."[5] And at a time when the Left was shocked that the police and military were spying on peace groups, far less attention was given to the government's continuing repression of the Puerto Rican liberation movement, including the FBI assassination of Machetero leader Filiberto Ojeda Ríos.[6]

But we need not infer the opinions and priorities of the state's security apparatus from the actions of its agents. We can take their word for it. FBI COINTELPRO documents, revealed to the public only because in 1971 some activists broke into an FBI office in Pennsylvania and stole them, clearly demonstrate that a major objective of the FBI is to keep would-be revolutionaries passive. In a list of five goals with regard to black nationalist and black liberation groups, in the 1960s, the FBI includes the following:

> Prevent violence on the part of black nationalist groups. This is of primary importance, and is, of course, a goal of our investigative activity; it should also be a goal of the Counterintelligence Program [in the original government lingo, that phrase refers to a specific operation, of which there were thousands, and not the overarching program]. Through counterintelligence it should be possible to pinpoint potential troublemakers and neutralize them before they exercise their potential for violence.[7]

In identifying successful "neutralizations" in other documents, the FBI uses the term to include activists who were assassinated, imprisoned, framed, discredited, or harassed until they ceased to be politically active. The memo also lists the importance of preventing the rise of a black "messiah." After smugly noting that Malcolm X could have fulfilled this role, but is instead the martyr of the movement, the memo names three black leaders who have the potential to be that messiah. One of the three "could be a very real contender for this position should he abandon his supposed 'obedience' to 'white, liberal doctrines' (nonviolence)" [parenthesis in the original]. The memo also explains the need to go about discrediting militant blacks in the eyes of the "responsible Negro community" and the "white community." This shows both how the state can count on knee-jerk pacifist condemnation of violence and how pacifists effectively do the state's work by failing to use their cultural influence to make militant resistance to tyranny "respectable." Instead, pacifists claim that militancy alienates people, and do nothing to attempt to counteract this phenomenon.

Another FBI memo, this one on American Indian Movement activist John Trudell, shows the same understanding on the part of the state's political police that pacifists are an inert sort of dissident that do not yet pose a threat to the established order. "TRUDELL has the ability to meet with a group of pacifists and in a short time have them yelling and screaming 'right-on!' In short, he is an extremely effective agitator."[8]

The government consistently demonstrates the unsurprising fact that it prefers to go up against a peaceful opposition. Much more recently, an FBI memo sent to local law-enforcement agencies across the country, and subsequently leaked to the press, makes it clear whom the government identifies as extremists and prioritizes for neutralization.

On October 25, 2003, mass marches and rallies against the occupation in Iraq are scheduled to occur in Washington, DC, and San Francisco, California....[T]he possibility exists that elements of the activist community may attempt to engage in violent, destructive, or disruptive acts....

Traditional demonstration tactics by which protestors draw attention to their causes include marches, banners, and forms of *passive* resistance such as sit-ins [emphasis mine]. Extremist elements may engage in more aggressive tactics that can include vandalism, physical harassment of delegates, trespassing, the formation of human chains or shields, makeshift barricades, devices used against mounted police units, and the use of weapons—such as projectiles and homemade bombs.[9]

The bulk of the memo focuses on these "extremist elements," clearly identified as activists employing a diversity of tactics, as opposed to pacifist activists, who are not identified as a major threat. According to the memo, extremists exhibit the following identifying characteristics.

Extremists may be prepared to defend themselves against law enforcement officials during the course of a demonstration. Masks (gas masks, goggles, scarves, scuba masks, filter masks, and sunglasses) can serve to minimize the effects of tear gas and pepper spray, as well as obscure one's identity. Extremists may also employ shields (trash can lids, sheets of plexiglass, truck tire inner tubes, etc.) and body protection equipment (layered clothing, hard hats and helmets, sporting equipment, life jackets, etc.) to protect themselves during marches. Activists may also use intimidation techniques such as videotaping and the swarming of police officers to hinder the arrest of other demonstrators.

After demonstrations, activists are usually reluctant to cooperate with law enforcement officials. They seldom carry any identification papers and often refuse to divulge any information about themselves or other protestors....

Law enforcement officials should be alert to these possible indicators of protest activity and report any potentially illegal acts to the nearest FBI Joint Terrorism Task Force.[10]

How sad is it that the surest mark of an "extremist" is a willingness to defend oneself against attacks by the police, and how much responsibility do pacifists bear in creating this situation? In any case, by disowning and even denouncing activists who use a diversity of tactics, pacifists make such extremists vulnerable to the repression that police agencies clearly want to use against them.

As if it were not enough to discourage militancy and condition dissidents to use nonviolence through violent repression of the unruly, the government also injects pacifism into rebel movements more directly. Two years after invading Iraq, the US military got caught interfering once again in the Iraqi news media (prior interference included bombing unfriendly media, releasing false stories, and creating entirely new Arab-language media organizations such as al-Hurriyah that would be run by the Defense Department as a part of their psychological operations). This time, the Pentagon was paying to insert articles in Iraqi newspapers urging unity (against the insurgents) and nonviolence.[11] The articles were written as though the authors were Iraqi in an attempt to rein in the militant resistance and manipulate Iraqis into diplomatic forms of opposition that would be easier to co-opt and control.

The Pentagon's selective use of pacifism in Iraq can serve as a parable for the broader origins of nonviolence. Namely, it comes from the state. A conquered population is schooled in nonviolence through its relationship with a power structure that has claimed a monopoly on the right to use violence. It is the acceptance, by the disempowered, of the statist belief that the masses must be stripped of their natural abilities for direct action, including the propensities for self-defense and the use of force, or they will descend into chaos, into a cycle of violence, into hurting and oppressing one another. Thus is government safety, and slavery freedom. Only a people trained to accept being ruled by a violent power structure can really question someone's right and need to forcefully defend herself against oppression. Pacifism is also a form of learned helplessness, through which dissidents retain the goodwill of the state by signifying that they have not usurped powers the state exclusively claims (such as self-defense). In this way, a pacifist behaves like a well-trained dog who is beaten by his master: rather than bite his attacker, he lowers his tail and signifies his harmlessness, resigning himself to the beatings in the hope that they stop.

More immediately, Frantz Fanon describes the origins and function of nonviolence within the decolonization process when he writes:

> The colonialist bourgeoisie] introduces that new idea which is in proper parlance a creation of the colonial situation: non-violence. In its simplest form this non-violence signifies to the intellectual and economic elite of the colonized country that the bourgeoisie has the same interests as they....Non-violence is an attempt to settle the colonial problem around a green baize table, before any regrettable act has been performed...before any blood has been shed. But if the masses, without waiting for the chairs to be arranged around the baize table, listen to their own voice and begin committing outrages and setting fire to buildings, the elite and the nationalist bourgeois parties will be seen rushing to the colonialists to exclaim, "This is very serious! We do not know how it will end; we must find a solution—some sort of compromise."[12]

This underlying comfort with the violence of the state, combined with shock at the "outrages" of forceful rebellion, lulls pacifists into relying on state violence for protection. For example, pacifist organizers exempt the police from the "nonviolence codes" that are common at protests these days; they do not attempt to disarm the police who protect peace protestors from angry, pro-war counterdemonstrators. In practice, pacifist morality demonstrates that it is more acceptable for radicals to rely on the violence of the government for protection than to defend themselves.

It is fairly obvious why the authorities would want radicals to remain vulnerable. But why do pacifists? It is not as though supporters of nonviolence have had a shortage of opportunities to learn what happens to defenseless radicals. Take for example the 1979 rally against white supremacy in Greensboro, North Carolina. An assortment of black and white workers, labor organizers, and Communists, accepting the premise that disarming and allowing a police monopoly on violent force would better ensure peace, agreed to not carry weapons for protection. The result was an event now known as the Greensboro Massacre. The police and FBI collaborated with the local Klan and Nazi Party to attack the demonstrators, who were relying on police protection. While the police were conveniently absent, the white supremacists attacked the march and shot 13 people, killing five. When the police re-turned to the scene, they beat and arrested several protestors and let the racist thugs get away.[13]

In the chaos of any revolutionary situation, right-wing para-militaries such as the Ku Klux Klan are more than happy to elimi-nate radicals. The American Legion recently declared "war" on the anti-war movement.[14] That organization's history of lynching anarchist labor organizers suggests the means they'll use when their beloved flag is threatened.[15]

The debate between pacifism and a diversity of tactics (in-cluding self-defense and counterattack) may end up being decided if the current anti-authoritarian movement ever develops to the point of posing a threat, when police agencies hand over their blacklists, and right-wing paramilitaries lynch any "traitors" they can get their hands on. This situation has occurred in the past, most notably in the 1920s, and, to a lesser extent, in response to the civil rights movement. Let us only hope that if our movement once again poses a threat, as few of us as possible will be con-strained by an ideology that leaves us dangerously vulnerable.

Despite this history of repression, proponents of nonviolence frequently rely on the violence of the state, not just to protect them, but also to accomplish their goals. If this reliance does not always lead to outright disasters like the Greensboro Massacre, it certainly cannot exonerate the nonviolent position. Pacifists claiming to eschew violence helped to desegregate schools and universities throughout the South, but, ultimately, it was armed units of the National Guard that allowed the first black students to enter these schools and protect them from forceful attempts at expulsion and worse. If pacifists are unable to defend their own gains, what will they do when they don't have the organized violence of the police and National Guard? (Incidentally, would pacifists remember desegregation as a failure for nonviolence if black families had needed to call in the Deacons for Defense, instead of the National Guard, to protect their children entering those all-white schools?) Institutional desegregation was deemed favorable to the white supremacist power structure because it defused a crisis, increased possibilities for co-opting black leadership, and streamlined the economy, all without negating the racial hierarchy so fundamental to US society. Thus, the National Guard was called in to help desegregate universities. It is not that hard to imagine a set of revolutionary goals that the National Guard would never be called in to protect.

While pacifists protesting US militarism can never get the police or National Guard to simply enforce the law—disarming weapons banned by international treaties or closing military schools that train soldiers in torture techniques—the government still benefits from allowing these futile demonstrations to take place. Permitting nonviolent protest improves the image of the state. Whether they mean to or not, nonviolent dissidents play the role of a loyal opposition in a performance that dramatizes dissent and creates the illusion that democratic government is not elitist or authoritarian. Pacifists paint the state as benign by giving authority the chance to tolerate a criticism that does not actually threaten its continued operation. A colorful, conscientious, passive protest in front of a military base only improves the PR image of the military, for surely only a just and humane military would tolerate protests outside its front gate. Such a protest is like a flower stuck in the barrel of a gun. It does not impede the ability of the gun to fire.

What most pacifists do not seem to understand is that free speech does not empower us, and it does not equal freedom. Free speech is a privilege[16] that can be—and is—taken away by the government when it serves their interests. The state has the uncontested power to take away our "rights," and history shows the exercise of that power regularly.[17] Even in our daily life, we can try to say whatever we want to bosses, judges, or police officers, and unless we are slavishly congenial, honesty and a free tongue will lead to harmful consequences. In situations of social emergency, the limitations on "free speech" become even more pronounced. Consider the activists imprisoned for speaking against the draft in World War I and the people arrested in 2004 for holding protest signs at events where Bush was speaking. Free speech is only free as long as it is not a threat and does not come with the possibility of challenging the system. The most freedom of speech I have ever had was in the "Security Housing Unit" (maximum-security solitary confinement) in federal prison. I could yell and shout all I wanted, even cuss at the guards, and unless I thought up a particularly creative way to intentionally enrage them, they would leave me at peace. No matter: the walls were rock solid and my words were hot air.

The cooperation that is only possible with peaceful dissidents helps to humanize the politicians responsible for monstrous policies. At the massive protests against the 2004 Republican National Convention (RNC) in New York City, NYC's Mayor Bloomberg gave special buttons to nonviolent activists who had proclaimed that they would be peaceful.[18] Bloomberg got political points for being hip and lenient, even as his administration cracked down on dissent during the week of protests. Pacifists got an added perk: anyone wearing the button would be given discounts at dozens of Broadway shows, hotels, museums, and restaurants (highlighting how the passive parade of nonviolence is tapped into as a boost to the economy and bulwark of the status quo). As Mayor Bloomberg put it, "It's no fun to protest on an empty stomach."

And the anti-RNC protests in New York were little more than that: fun. Fun for college students, Democratic canvassers, and Green Party activists to walk around holding witty signs with like-minded "enlightened" progressives. A huge amount of energy was expended weeks in advance (by the institutional Left and the police) in attempts to alienate and exclude more militant activists. Someone with a lot of resources distributed thousands of leaflets the weekend before the convention making the idiotic claim that violence—say, a riot—would improve Bush's image (when, in reality, a riot, though it certainly would not have helped the Democrats, would have tarnished Bush's image as a leader and "uniter"). The leaflet also warned that anyone advocating confrontational tactics was likely a police agent. The march ended, and people dispersed to the most isolated, least confrontational spot possible in a city full of the edifices of state and capital: Central Park's Grand Lawn (appropriately, other protestors flocked to the "Sheep Meadow"). They danced and celebrated into the night, chanting such illuminating mantras as "We are beautiful!"

Later in the week, the Poor People's March was repeatedly attacked by police making targeted arrests of activists wearing masks or refusing to be searched. March participants had agreed to be nonviolent because the march included many people, such as immigrants and people of color, whom march organizers were ostensibly concerned about as being more vulnerable to arrest. But when activists—peacefully—swarmed police officers to attempt to discourage the arrests, the activists were urged to ignore the arrests and keep moving, with march "peacekeepers" and police shouting identical messages at the crowd ("Move along!" "Stick to the march route!"). Obviously, all attempts at conciliation and de-escalation failed; the police were every bit as violent as they chose to be.

The next day, Jamal Holiday, a black New York City resident from a disadvantaged background, was arrested for the self-defense "assault" of a plainclothes NYPD detective, one of several who had, with no provocation, driven their mopeds into the peaceful crowd at the Poor People's March, hurting several people (and running over my foot). This happened at the end of the rally, when many of the march participants, including the supposedly "vulnerable," were quite upset with the march leaders' passivity and the continued police brutality. At one point, a crowd of protestors who had just been attacked by police began screaming at an organizer who was yelling at them through a bullhorn to get away from the police (there was nowhere to go) because they were "provoking" the cops. The response to Holiday's arrest shows a hypocrisy that privileges state violence over even the right of people to defend themselves. The same pacifist segments of the movement who raised a stink about the peaceful protestors whom police arrested en masse on August 31 (a day reserved for civil disobedience–style protests) remained silent toward and unsupportive of Holiday while he endured the excruciating, drawn-out violence of the penal system. Apparently, for the pacifists, protecting an allegedly violent activist from a far greater violence comes too near to blurring their principled stand against violence.

Nonviolent activists go further than endorsing state violence with their silence: they are often vocal in justifying it. Pacifist organizers waste no opportunity to declare a ban on "violence" within their protests, because such violence would "justify" repression by the police, which is perceived as inevitable, neutral, and beyond reproach. The 1999 anti-WTO protests in Seattle are a typical example. Though police violence (in this case, the use of torture tactics against peaceful protestors blockading the summit site) preceded the "violent" property destruction by the black bloc, everyone from pacifists to the corporate media blamed the police riot on the black bloc. Perhaps the major grievance was that decentralized, non-hierarchically organized anarchists stole the spotlight from big-budget NGOs that require an aura of authority to keep receiving donations. The official claim was that the violence of the protests demonized the entire movement, though even the president himself, Bill Clinton, declared from Seattle that a violent fringe minority was solely responsible for the mayhem.[19] In fact, the violence of Seattle intrigued and attracted more new people to the movement than were attracted by the tranquility of any subsequent mass mobilization. The corporate media did not—and never will—explain the motives of the activists, but the violence, the visible manifestation of passion and fury, of militant commitment in an otherwise absurd world, motivated thousands to do that research on their own. That is why Seattle is thought of by the ahistorical as the "beginning" or "birth" of the anti-globalization movement.

Similarly, an article advocating nonviolence in *The Nation* complains that violence in Seattle and Genoa (where Italian police shot and killed a protestor) "created negative media images and provided an excuse for even harsher repression."[20] I will digress for a moment here to point out that the state is not a passive thing. If it wants to repress a movement or organization, it does not wait for an excuse, it manufactures one. The American Indian Movement was not a violent organization—the vast majority of its tactics were peaceful—but members did not restrict themselves to nonviolence; they practiced armed self-defense and forceful occupations of government buildings, often with great results. To "justify" repression against AIM, the FBI manufactured the "Dog Soldier Teletypes," which were passed off as AIM communiqués discussing the supposed creation of terror squads to assassinate tourists, farmers, and government officials.[21] These teletypes were part of a general FBI disinformation campaign instrumental in allowing the consequence-free (for the government) false imprisonment and murder of several AIM activists and supporters. About such campaigns, the FBI says, "It is immaterial whether facts exist to substantiate the charge....[D]isruption [through the media] can be accomplished without facts to back it up."[22] If, in the eyes of the government, it is immaterial whether an organization deemed a threat to the status quo has or has not committed a violent act, why do proponents of nonviolence continue to insist that the truth will set them free?

The previously mentioned *Nation* article demands a strict, movement-wide adherence to nonviolence, criticizing another pacifist organization's refusal to openly condemn activists who use a diversity of tactics. The author laments, "It's impossible to control the actions of everyone who participates in a demonstration, of course, but more vigorous efforts to insure [*sic*] nonviolence and prevent destructive behavior are possible and necessary. A 95 percent commitment to nonviolence is not enough." No doubt, a "more vigorous" commitment to nonviolence means that activist leaders must more frequently utilize the police as a force for peace (to arrest "troublemakers"). This tactic has most certainly been applied by pacifists already. (In fact, the first time I ever got assaulted at a protest, it was not by the police but by a peace marshal, who tried to push me to the curb while I and several others were holding an intersection to keep the police from dividing the march and potentially mass-arresting the smaller segment. Notably, my resistance to the peace marshal's light attempts to push me back visibly singled me out to the police, who were overseeing the work of their proxies, and I had to duck back into the crowd to avoid being arrested or assaulted more forcefully.)

Can anyone imagine revolutionary activists declaring that they need to be more vigorous in making sure that every participant in an event hits a cop or throws a brick through a window? On the contrary, most anarchists and other militants have bent over backwards in working with pacifists and ensuring that at joint demonstrations, people opposed to confrontation, afraid of police brutality, or especially vulnerable to legal sanctions could have a "safe space." Pacifism goes hand in hand with efforts to centralize and control the movement. The concept is inherently authoritarian and incompatible with anarchism because it denies people the right to self-determination in directing their own struggles.[23] The pacifist reliance on centralization and control (with a leadership that can take "vigorous efforts" to "prevent destructive behavior") preserves the state within the movement, and preserves hierarchical structures to assist state negotiations (and state repression).

History shows that if a movement does not have a leader, the state invents one. The state violently eliminated the anti-hierarchical labor unions of the early 20th century, whereas it negotiated with, elevated, and bought off the leadership of the hierarchical unions. Colonial regimes appointed "chiefs" to stateless societies that had none, whether to impose political control in Africa or negotiate deceptive treaties in North America. Additionally, leaderless social movements are especially hard to repress. The tendencies of pacifism toward negotiation and centralization facilitate efforts by the state to manipulate and co-opt rebellious social movements; they also make it easier for the state to repress a movement, if it decides there is a need to do so.

But the pacifist vision of social change comes from a privileged vantage, where full state repression is not a real fear. An essay on strategic nonviolence that came highly recommended from some pacifist acquaintances includes a diagram. Nonviolent activists are on the left, their opponents, presumably reactionaries, are on the right, and undecided third parties are in the middle.[24] All three segments are equally arrayed around an apparently neutral "decision-making" authority. This is an utterly naive and privileged view of democratic government, in which all decisions are decided by majority, with, at worst, a limited violence practiced only out of recalcitrant conservatism and reluctance to change the status quo. The diagram assumes a society without race and class hierarchy; without privileged, powerful, and violent elites; without a corporate media controlled by the interests of state and capital, ready to manage the perceptions of the citizenry. Such a society does not exist among any of the industrial, capitalist democracies.

Within such a model of social power, revolution is a morality play, an advocacy campaign that can be won by "the ability of dignified suffering [for example, the anti-segregation students sitting in at "whites only" lunch counters while enduring verbal and physical attacks] to attract sympathy and political support."[25] First of all, this model assumes an analysis of the state that is remarkably charitable and remarkably similar to how the state might describe itself in public-school civics textbooks. In this analysis, government is a neutral and passive decision-making authority that responds to public pressures. It is at best fair and at worst beset by a culture of conservatism and ignorance. But it is not structurally oppressive. Second, this model puts pacifists in the position of pressuring and negotiating with a decision-making authority that, in reality, is consciously bound by self-interest, willing to break any inconvenient law it may have set down, and structurally integrated with and dependent on the systems of power and oppression that galvanized the social movement in the first place.

Modern governments, which have long studied methods of social control, no longer view peace as the default social condition, interrupted only by outside agitators. Now they understand that the natural condition of the world (the world they have created, I should editorialize) is conflict: rebellion to their rule is inevitable and continuous.[26] Statecraft has become the art of managing conflict, permanently. As long as rebels continue to carry olive branches and a naive view of the struggle, the state knows that it is safe. But the same governments whose representatives hold polite talks with or rudely dismiss conscientious hunger strikers also constantly spy on the resistance and train agents in counterinsurgency-warfare techniques drawn from wars of extermination waged to subdue rebellious colonies from Ireland to Algeria. The state is prepared to use those methods against us.

Even when the government stops short of exterminatory forms of repression, dignified suffering simply stops being fun, and pacifists who have not fully dedicated their futures to revolution by declaring war on the status quo lose the clarity of conviction (maybe they somehow did something to "deserve" or "provoke" the repression?) and drop out. Consider the 1999 Seattle protest and the successive mass mobilizations of the anti-globalization movement: activists in Seattle were brutalized, but they took it on their feet, fighting back, and many were empowered by the experience. The same goes for the Quebec City demonstrations against the Free Trade Area of Americas (FTAA). At the other end, police repression at the 2003 anti-FTAA protests in Miami was wholly undeserved even by legalistic standards.[27] Protestors were not empowered or dignified by the one-sided violence—they were brutalized, and many people were scared away from further participation, including activists who were sexually assaulted by police while locked up. In the even more passive protests in Washington, DC—the yearly demonstrations against the World Bank, for instance—nonviolent resistance, consisting of the occasional orchestrated lockdown, arrest, imprisonment, and release, were not empowering so much as tedious and marked by dwindling numbers. They were certainly not successful in winning media attention or influencing people with the spectacle of dignified suffering, though in every case the criteria used by the pacifist organizers to ascertain victory was a combination of nothing more than the numbers of participants and the absence of violent confrontation with authorities or property.

In the final analysis, the state can use nonviolence to defeat even a revolutionary movement that has otherwise become powerful enough to succeed. In Albania in 1997, government corruption and economic collapse caused a large number of families to lose all their savings. In response, the "Socialist Party called a demonstration in the capital hoping to make itself the leader of a peaceful protest movement."[28] But the resistance spread far beyond the control of any political party. People began arming themselves; burning or bombing banks, police stations, government buildings, and offices of the secret service; and liberating prisons. "Much of the military deserted, either joining the insurgents or fleeing to Greece." The Albanian people were poised to overthrow the system that was oppressing them, which would give them a chance to create new social organizations for themselves. "By mid-March, the government, including the secret police, was forced to flee the capital." Soon after, several thousand European Union troops occupied Albania to restore central authority. The opposition parties, which all along had been negotiating with the government to find a set of conditions to induce the rebels to disarm and convince the ruling party to step down (so they could step up), were instrumental in allowing the occupation to pacify the rebels, conduct elections, and reinstitute the state.

Similarly, Frantz Fanon describes opposition parties that denounced violent rebellion in the colonies out of a desire to control the movement. "After the first skirmishes, the official leaders speedily dispose of" militant action, which they "label as childishness." Then, "the revolutionary elements which subscribe to them will rapidly be isolated. The official leaders, draped in their years of experience, will pitilessly disown these 'adventurers and anarchists.'" As Fanon explains, regarding Algeria, in particular, and anti-colonial struggles, in general, "The party machine shows itself opposed to any innovation," and the leaders "are terrified and worried by the idea that they could be swept away by a maelstrom whose nature, force, or direction they cannot even imagine."[29] Though these oppositional political leaders, whether in Albania, Algeria, or elsewhere, generally do not identify as pacifists, it is interesting to note how they play a similar role. For their part, genuine pacifists are more likely to accept the deceptive olive branches of pacifying politicians than offers of solidarity from armed revolutionaries. The standard alliance and fraternizing between pacifists and progressive political leaders (who counsel moderation) serve to fracture and control revolutionary movements. It is in the absence of significant pacifist penetration into popular movements that political leaders fail to control those movements and are rejected and amputated as elitist leeches. It is when nonviolence is tolerated by popular movements that these movements are hamstrung.

In the end, nonviolent activists rely on the violence of the state to protect their gains, and they do not resist the violence of the state when it is used against militants (in fact, they often encourage it). They negotiate and cooperate with armed police at their demonstrations. And, though pacifists honor their "prisoners of conscience," in my experience, they tend to ignore the violence of the prison system in cases where the prisoner committed an act of violent resistance or even vandalism (not to mention an apolitical crime). When I was serving a six-month prison sentence for an act of civil disobedience, pacifists across the country flooded me with support. But, on the whole, they show a lack of concern for the institutionalized violence encaging the 2.2 million casualties of the government's War on Crime. It seems that the only form of violence they consistently oppose is rebellion against the state.

The peace sign itself is the perfect metaphor for this function. Instead of raising a fist, pacifists raise their index and middle fingers to form a V. That V stands for *victory* and is the symbol of patriots exulting in the peace that follows a triumphant war. In the final analysis, the peace that pacifists defend is that of the vanquishing army, the unopposed state that has conquered all resistance and monopolized violence to such an extent that violence need no longer be visible. It is a Pax Americana.

4

Patriarchy is a form of social organization that produces what we commonly recognize as sexism. But it goes well beyond individual or systemic prejudice against women. It is, first of all, the false division of all people into two rigid categories (male and female) that are asserted to be both natural and moral. (Many perfectly healthy people do not fit into either of these physiological categories, and many non-Western cultures recognized—and still do, if they haven't been destroyed—more than two sexes and genders.) Patriarchy attempts to destroy, socially or even physically, anyone who does not fit into one of these two categories or who rejects this "gender binary." Patriarchy goes on to define clear roles (economic, social, emotional, political) for men and women, and it asserts (falsely) that these roles are natural and moral. Under patriarchy, people who do not fit into or who reject these gender roles are neutralized with violence and ostracism. They are made to seem and feel ugly, dirty, scary, contemptible, worthless. Patriarchy is harmful to everybody, and it is reproduced by everyone who lives within it. True to its name, it puts men in a dominant position and women in a submissive position. Activities and characteristics that are traditionally associated with "power," or, at least privilege, mostly belong to men.[1] Patriarchy gives both the ability and the right to use violence almost exclusively to men.

With gender, as with race, nonviolence is an inherently privileged position. Nonviolence assumes that instead of defending ourselves against violence, we can suffer violence patiently until enough of society can be mobilized to oppose it peacefully (or that we can expect to "transform" any aggression that threatens us individually). Most proponents of nonviolence will present it as not merely a narrow political practice but a philosophy that deserves to penetrate the very social fabric and root out violence in all its manifestations. But pacifists seem not to have given the violence of patriarchy its due consideration. After all, in wars, in social revolutions, and in daily life, women and transgender people are the primary recipients of violence in patriarchal society.

If we take this philosophy out of the impersonal political arena and put it in a more real context, nonviolence implies that it is immoral for a woman to fight off an attacker or study self-defense. Nonviolence implies that it is better for an abused wife to move out than to mobilize a group of women to beat up and kick out her abusive husband.[2] Nonviolence implies that it is better for someone to be raped than to pull the mechanical pencil out of her pocket and plunge it into her assailant's jugular (because doing so would supposedly contribute to some cycle of violence and encourage future rapes). Pacifism simply does not resonate in people's everyday realities, unless those people live in some extravagant bubble of tranquility from which all forms of civilization's pandemic reactive violence have been pushed out by the systemic and less visible violence of police and military forces.

From another angle, nonviolence seems well-suited to dealing with patriarchy. After all, the abolition of patriarchy in particular requires forms of resistance that emphasize healing and reconciliation.[3] The Western concept of justice, based on law and punishment, is patriarchal through and through. Early legal codes defined women as property, and laws were written for male property owners, who had been socialized not to deal with emotions; "wrongs" were addressed through punishment rather than reconciliation. Furthermore, patriarchy is not upheld by a powerful elite who must be forcibly defeated, but by everyone.

Because the distribution of power within patriarchy is much more diffused than within the state or capitalism (for example, a male general who also sits on the advisory board of a major corporation holds significant power within the state and capitalism, but does not derive much more power specifically from patriarchy than any other male, except perhaps as a role model of manliness), fighting against power holders or those most responsible plays a much smaller role. Instead, people must build a culture that allows everyone to self-identify in terms of gender and that supports us as we build healthy relationships and heal from generations of violence and trauma. This is perfectly compatible with self-defense training for women and transgender people and attacks on economic, cultural, and political institutions that exemplify patriarchy or are responsible for an especially brutal form of it. Killing a cop who rapes homeless transgender people and prostitutes, burning down the office of a magazine that consciously markets a beauty standard that leads to anorexia and bulimia, kidnapping the president of a company that conducts women-trafficking—none of these actions prevent the building of a healthy culture. Rather, certain powerful people who consciously profit from patriarchy actively prevent a healthy culture from emerging. Valuing healthy relationships is complemented by militantly opposing institutions that propagate exploitive and violent relationships, and striking out against the most egregious and probably incorrigible examples of patriarchy is one way to educate others about the need for an alternative. Most of the work needed to overcome patriarchy will probably be peaceful, focused on healing and building alternatives. But a pacifist practice that forbids the use of any other tactics leaves no option for people who need to protect themselves from violence now.

In the case of rape and other forms of violence against women, nonviolence implies the same lessons that patriarchy has taught for millennia. It glorifies passivity, "turning the other cheek," and "dignified suffering" among the oppressed. In one of the most lucid texts defining the preservation and implementation of patriarchy—the Old Testament—story upon commandment upon parable upon law counsel women to suffer injustice patiently and pray for the divine Authority to intervene. (This prescription is remarkably similar to pacifists' faith in the corporate media to disseminate images of dignified suffering and motivate the "decision-making authority" to implement justice). Because patriarchy clearly prescribes a one-sided male violence, women would be disrupting this power dynamic, not reinforcing it, by relearning their propensity for violence.[4] To reiterate, women reclaiming the ability and right to use force would not by itself end patriarchy, but it is a necessary condition for gender liberation, as well as a useful form of empowerment and protection in the short term.

Pacifists and reformist feminists have often charged that it is militant activists who are sexist. In many specific cases, the accusation has been valid. But the criticism is frequently broadened to suggest that the use of violent activism itself is sexist, masculine, or otherwise privileged.[5] As Laina Tanglewood explains, "Some recent 'feminist' critiques of anarchism have condemned militancy as being sexist and non-inclusive to women....This idea is actually the sexist one."[6] Another anarchist points out, "In fact, the masculinization of violence, with its unstated sexist concomitant, the feminization of passivity, really owes more to the presumptions of those whose notion of change does not include revolution or the annihilation of the State."[7]

Likewise, whose notion of freedom does not include women's being able to defend themselves? Responding to the presumption that women can only be protected by larger social structures, activist Sue Daniels reminds us, "A woman can fight off a male attacker by herself....It is absolutely not a question of who is physically stronger—it is a question of training."[8] "The Will to Win! Women and Self-Defense," an anonymously authored pamphlet, adds the following:

> It is ridiculous that there are so many counseling and support organizations for women who have been raped, attacked, and abused but hardly any that work to prepare and prevent these things from happening. We must refuse to be victims and reject the idea that we should submit to our

assailants to keep from arousing further violence. In reality, submitting to our assailants will only contribute to future violence against others.[9]

The entire idea that violence is masculine, or that revolutionary activism necessarily excludes women, queers, and trans people is, like other premises of nonviolence, based on historical whitewashing. Ignored are the Nigerian women occupying and sabotaging petroleum facilities; the women martyrs of the Palestinian intifada; the queer and transgender warriors of the Stonewall Rebellion; the innumerable thousands of women who fought for the Vietcong; women leaders of Native resistance to European and US genocide; Mujeres Creando (Women Creating), a group of anarcha-feminists in Bolivia; and British suffragettes who rioted and fought against cops. Forgotten are the women from the rank and file to the highest levels of leadership among the Black Panther Party, the Zapatistas, the Weather Underground, and other militant groups. The idea that fighting back somehow excludes women is absurd. Not even the history of the pacified white "First World" bears it up because even the most effective patriarchy imaginable could never prevent all transgender people and all women from militantly fighting against oppression.

Advocates of nonviolence who make a limited exception for self-defense because they recognize how wrong it is to say that oppressed people cannot or should not protect themselves have no viable strategies for dealing with systemic violence. Is it self-defense to fight off an abusive husband, but not to blow up a dioxin-emitting factory that is making your breast milk toxic? What about a more concerted campaign to destroy the corporation that owns the factory and is responsible for releasing the pollutants? Is it self-defense to kill the general who sends out the soldiers who rape women in a war zone? Or must pacifists remain on the defensive, only fighting individual attacks and submitting themselves to the inevitability of such attacks until nonviolent tactics somehow convert the general or close down the factory, at some uncertain point in the future?

Aside from protecting the patriarchy from militant opposition, nonviolence also helps preserve patriarchal dynamics within the movement. One of the major premises of current anti-oppression activism (born out of the joint desire to promote healthier, more empowered movements and to avoid the infighting which stemmed largely from neglected oppressive dynamics that crippled the previous generation's liberation struggles) is that oppressive social hierarchies exist and replicate themselves in the behavior of all subjects and must be overcome internally as well as externally. But pacifism thrives on avoiding self-criticism.[10] Many are familiar with the partially justified stereotype of self-congratulatory, self-celebratory nonviolent activists who "embody the change [they] wish to see in the world"[11] to such a degree that in their minds, they embody everything right and beautiful. A follower in one pacifist organization exclaimed, in response to criticisms of privilege, that the group's white, male leader could not possibly have white privilege and male privilege because he was such a good person, as though white supremacy and patriarchy were entirely voluntary associations.[12] In such a context, how easily could a predominantly male leadership that is understood to embody the nonviolent ideal as a result of their participation in an impressive number of hunger strikes and sit-ins be called out for oppressive behavior, transphobia, or sexual abuse?

The pacifist avoidance of self-criticism is functional, not just typical. When your strategy's victory comes from "captur[ing] and maintain[ing] the moral high ground,"[13] it is necessary to portray yourself as moral and your enemy as immoral. Uncovering bigotries and oppressive dynamics among group leaders and members is simply counterproductive to your chosen strategy. How many people know that Martin Luther King Jr. treated Ella Baker (who is largely responsible for building the foundation of the Southern Christian Leadership Conference [SCLC] while King was still inexperienced as an organizer) like his secretary; laughed in the faces of several women in the organization when they suggested that power and leadership should be shared; said that women's natural role was motherhood, and that they, unfortunately, were "forced" into the positions of "teacher" and "leader";[14] and removed Bayard Rustin from his organization because Rustin was gay?[15] But then, why would these facts be widely available when making an icon of King entailed covering up any such faults and portraying him as a saint? For *revolutionary* activists, however, victory comes from building power and out-strategizing the state. Such a path requires constant assessment and self-criticism.[16]

It is often preexisting sexist assumptions that paint militant groups as more sexist than they actually are. For example, women were effectively excluded from leadership positions in King's SCLC,[17] whereas women (for example, Elaine Brown) at times held the top positions in the Black Panther Party (BPP). Yet it is the BPP, and not the SCLC, that is held up as the paragon of machismo. Kathleen Cleaver rebuts, "In 1970, the Black Panther Party took a formal position on the liberation of women. Did the US Congress ever make any statement on the liberation of women?"[18] Frankye Malika Adams, another Panther, said, "Women ran the BPP pretty much. I don't know how it got to be a male's party or thought of as being a male's party."[19] In resurrecting a truer history of the Black Panther Party, Mumia Abu-Jamal documents what was, in some ways, "a woman's party."[20]

Nonetheless, sexism persisted among the Panthers, as it persists within any revolutionary milieu, and any other segment of a patriarchal society today. Patriarchy cannot be destroyed overnight, but it can be gradually overcome by groups that work to destroy it. Activists must recognize patriarchy as a primary enemy and open spaces within revolutionary movements for women, queer people, and transgender people to be creative forces in directing, assessing, and reformulating the struggle (while also supporting men's efforts to understand and counter our own socialization). An honest evaluation shows that no matter our intentions, more work remains to be done to free control of the movement from the hands of men and to find healthy, restorative ways to deal with abusive patterns in relationships, social or romantic, among members of the movement.

Whether militant or pacifist, nearly every tactical or strategic discussion I have participated in was attended and dominated overwhelmingly by men. Rather than claim that women and transgender people are somehow unable to participate in a broad spectrum of tactical options (or even discuss them), we would do well to recall the voices of those who have fought—violently, defiantly, effectively—as revolutionaries. To that end:

Mujeres Creando is an anarcha-feminist group in Bolivia. Its members have engaged in graffiti campaigns and anti-poverty campaigns. They protect protestors from police violence at demonstrations. In their most dramatic action, they armed themselves with Molotov cocktails and sticks of dynamite and helped a group of indigenous farmers take over a bank to demand forgiveness of the debt that was starving the farmers and their families. In an interview, Julieta Paredes, a founding member, explains the group's origins.

> Mujeres Creando is a "craziness" started by three women [Julieta Paredes, Maria Galindo, and Monica Mendoza] from the arrogant, homophobic, and totalitarian Left of Bolivia of the '80s....The difference between us and those who talk about the overthrow of capitalism is that all their proposals for a new society come from the patriarchy of the Left. As feminists in Mujeres Creando we want revolution, a real change of the system....I've said it and I'll say it again that we're not anarchists by Bakunin or the CNT, but rather by our grandmothers, and that's a beautiful school of anarchism."[21]

Sylvia Rivera, a Puerto Rican drag queen, talked about her participation in the 1969 Stonewall Rebellion, sparked after police raided the Stonewall Bar in New York City's Greenwich Village to harass the queer and trans patrons.

We were not taking any more of this shit. We had done so much for other movements. It was time.

It was street gay people from the Village out front—homeless people who lived in the park in Sheridan Square outside the bar—and then drag queens behind them and everybody behind us....

I'm glad I was in the Stonewall Riot. I remember when someone threw a Molotov cocktail, I thought: "My god, the revolution is here. The revolution is finally here!"

I always believed that we would have a fight back. I just knew that we would fight back. I just didn't know it would be that night. I am proud of myself as being there that night. If I had lost that moment, I would have been kind of hurt because that's when I saw the world change for me and my people.

Of course, we still got a long way ahead of us.[22]

Ann Hansen is a Canadian revolutionary who served seven years in prison for her involvement in the 1980s with the underground groups Direct Action and the Wimmin's Fire Brigade, which (among other actions) bombed the factory of Litton Systems (a manufacturer of cruise-missile components) and firebombed a chain of pornography shops that sold videos depicting rapes. According to Hansen:

There are many different forms of direct action, some more effective than others at different points in history, but in conjunction with other forms of protest, direct action can make the movement for change more effective by opening avenues of resistance that are not easily co-opted or controlled by the state. Unfortunately, people within the movement weaken their own actions by failing to understand and support the diverse tactics available....We have become pacified.[23]

Russian-born Emma Goldman—America's most famous anarchist, participant in the attempted assassination of steel boss

Henry Clay Frick in 1892, supporter of the Russian Revolution, and one of the earliest critics of the Leninist government—writes of women's emancipation, "History tells us that every oppressed class gained true liberation from its masters through its own efforts. It is necessary that woman learn that lesson, that she realize that her freedom will reach as far as her power to achieve freedom reaches."[24]

Mollie Steimer was another Russian-American immigrant anarchist. From a young age, Steimer worked with *Frayhayt*, a Yiddish-language anarchist paper from New York. Its masthead proclaimed: "The only just war is the social revolution." From 1918 onwards, Steimer was arrested and imprisoned repeatedly for speaking out against the First World War or in support of the Russian Revolution, which, at that time, before the Leninist consolidation and purges, had a significant anarchist component. At one trial she declared, "To the fulfillment of this idea [anarchism], I will devote all my energy, and, if necessary, render my life for it."[25] Steimer was deported to Russia and then jailed by the Soviets for supporting anarchist prisoners there.

Anna Mae Pictou-Aquash was a Mi'kmaq woman and American Indian Movement (AIM) activist. After teaching, counseling Native youth, and "working with Boston's African American and Native American communities,"[26] she joined AIM and was involved in the 71-day occupation of Wounded Knee on the Pine Ridge Reservation in 1973. In 1975, at the height of a period of brutal state repression during which at least 60 AIM members and supporters were murdered by paramilitaries equipped by the FBI, Pictou-Aquash was present at a shoot-out in which two FBI agents were killed. In November 1975, she was declared a fugitive for avoiding court appearances on explosives charges. In February 1976, she was found dead, shot in the back of the head; the state coroner listed the cause of death as "exposure." After her death, it was learned that the FBI had threatened her life for not selling out other AIM activists. During her life, Pictou-Aquash was an outspoken activist and revolutionary.

These white people think this country belongs to them—they do not realize that they are only in charge right now because there are more of them than there are of us. The whole country changed with only a handful of raggedy-ass pilgrims that came over here in the 1500s. It can take a handful of raggedy-ass Indians to do the same, and I intend to be one of those raggedy-ass Indians."[27]

Rote Zora (RZ) was a German urban guerrilla group of anti-imperialist feminists. Together with the allied Revolutionary Cells, they carried out more than two hundred attacks, mostly bombings, during the 1970s and 80s. They targeted pornographers; corporations using sweatshops; government buildings; companies trading women as wives, sex slaves, and domestic workers; drug companies; and more. In an anonymous interview, Rote Zora members explained that: "the women of RZ started in 1974 with the bombing of the Supreme Court in Karlsruhe because we all wanted the total abolishment of '218' (the abortion law)."[28] Asked whether violence such as their bombings harms the movement, the members replied:

Zora 1: To harm the movement—you talk about the installation of repression. The actions don't harm the movement! It's the opposite, they should and can support the movement directly. Our attack on the women traders, for example, helped to expose their business to the public light, to threaten them, and they now know they have to anticipate the resistance of women if they go on with their business. These "gentlemen" know they have to anticipate resistance. We call this a strengthening of our movement.

Zora 2: For a long time the strategy of counter-revolution has begun to split the radical wing from the rest of the movement by any means and isolate them to weaken the whole movement. In the '70s we had the experience of what it means when sectors of the Left adopt the propaganda of the state, when they start to present those who struggle uncompromisingly as responsible for state persecution, destruction, and repression. They not only confuse cause with effect, but also justify implicitly state terror. Therefore, they weaken their own position. They narrow the frame of their protest and their resistance....

The interview went on to ask the following question.

How can non-autonomous, non-radical women understand what you want? Armed actions do have a "scare away" effect.

Zora 2: Maybe it is scary if everyday reality is questioned. Women who get it pounded into their heads from the time they are little girls that they are victims get insecure if they are confronted with the fact that women are neither victims nor peaceful. This is a provocation. Those women who experience their powerlessness with rage can identify with our actions. As every act of violence against one woman creates an atmosphere of threat against all women—our actions contribute—even if they aim only against the individual responsible—to the development of an atmosphere of "Resistance is possible!"[29]

There is, however, a great deal of feminist literature that denies the empowering (and historically important) effects of militant struggle on women's and other movements, offering instead a pacifist feminism. Pacifist feminists point to the sexism and machismo of certain militant liberation organizations, which we should all acknowledge and address. Arguing against nonviolence and in favor of a diversity of tactics should not at all imply a satisfaction with the strategies or cultures of past militant groups (for example, the macho posturing of the Weather Underground or the anti-feminism of the Red Brigades).[30] But taking these criticisms seriously should not prevent us from pointing out the hypocrisy of feminists who gladly decry sexist behavior by militants but cover it up when it is committed by pacifists—for example, relishing the tale that Gandhi learned nonviolence from his wife without mentioning the disturbingly patriarchal aspects of their relationship.[31]

Some feminists go further than specific criticisms and attempt to forge a metaphysical link between feminism and nonviolence: this is the "feminization of passivity" mentioned earlier. In an article published in the Berkeley journal *Peace Power,* Carol Flinders cites a study by UCLA scientists asserting that women are hormonally programmed to respond to danger not with the fight-or-flight mechanism, which is ascribed to men, but with a "tend or befriend" mechanism. When threatened, according to these scientists, women will "quiet the children, feed everyone, defuse the tension, and connect with other females."[32] This sort of pop science has long been a favored tool to reconstitute the patriarchy by supposedly proving the existence of natural differences between men and women, and people are all too willing to forget basic mathematic principles in order to surrender to such a well-ordered world. Namely, arbitrarily dividing humanity into two sets (male and female) based on a very limited number of characteristics will invariably produce different averages for each set. People who do not know that an average does not express, but obscures, the diversity within a set happily declare these two sets to be natural categories and continue to make people feel like they are unnatural and abnormal if they do not fall close to the average of their set (God forbid they fall closer to the average of the other set. Let's pause for a moment to drink a toast to the impartiality of Science!)

But Flinders is not content to pause there, with the implicitly transphobic and gender-essentializing[33] UCLA study. She goes on to delve into "our remote, pre-human past. Among chimpanzees, our nearest relations, males patrol the territory within which the females and infants feed....Females are rarely out on those frontlines; they're more typically engaged in direct care of their offspring." Flinders asserts that this shows "it's never been particularly adaptive for women to engage in direct combat" and "women tend to come at [nonviolence] from a somewhat different direction and even live it out rather differently."[34] Flinders is committing another scientific blunder, and has taken on a remarkably sexist tone. Firstly, the evolutionary determinism she is using is neither scrupulous nor proven—its popularity comes from its utility in creating an alibi for oppressive historical social structures. Even within this dubious framework, Flinders is flawed in her assumptions. Humans did not evolve from chimpanzees; rather, both species evolved from the same predecessor. Chimpanzees are every bit as modern as humans, and both species have had the opportunity to evolve behavioral adaptations that diverge from the common ancestor. We are not bound to the gender divisions of chimps any more than they are bound to our propensity for developing immense vocabularies to obscure the truth of the world around us. Secondly, along the same path that has brought her to assert a female tendency toward nonviolence, Flinders has run into the assertion that women's natural role is comforting children and feeding everybody—away from the frontlines. Flinders has boldly, albeit accidentally, demonstrated that the same belief system that says women are peaceful also says women's role is to cook and raise children. The name of that belief system is patriarchy.

Another article by a feminist academic waxes essentialist right off the bat. In the second paragraph of "Feminism and Nonviolence: A Relational Model," Patrizia Longo writes:

> Years of research...suggest that despite the potential problems involved, women consistently participate in nonviolent action. However, women choose nonviolence not because they wish to improve themselves through additional suffering, but because the strategy fits their values and resources.[35]

In constraining women to nonviolence, it seems that pacifist feminists must also constrain our definition of women's "values and resources," thus defining which traits are essentially feminine, locking women into a role that is falsely named natural, and shutting out people who do not fit that role.

It is hard to tell how many feminists today accept the premises of essentialism, but it seems that a large number of rank-and-file feminists do not accept the idea that feminism and nonviolence are or must be inherently linked. On one discussion board, dozens of self-identified feminists responded to the question, Is there a link between nonviolence and feminism? A majority of respondents, some pacifist, many not, expressed the belief that feminists do not need to support nonviolence. One message summed it up: "There is still a substantial strain in feminism that links women with nonviolence. But there are also a lot of feminists out there, myself included, who don't want to see ourselves automatically linked to one stance (that is, nonviolence) merely because of our genitalia or our feminism."[36]

Nonviolent activists attempting to appear strategic often avoid any real strategizing with intrepid simplitudes such as "Violence is the government's strong suit. We need to follow the path of least resistance and hit them where they're weak."[1] It's high time to make the distinction between strategizing and sloganeering, and get a little more sophisticated.

5

NONVIOLENCE IS TACTICALLY AND STRATEGICALLY INFERIOR

First, let's start with some definitions. (The usages I will give for the following terms are not universal, but as long as we use them consistently they will be more than adequate for our purposes.) A strategy is not a goal, a slogan, or an action. Violence is not a strategy, and neither is nonviolence. These two terms (*violence* and *nonviolence*) ostensibly are boundaries placed around sets of tactics. A limited set of tactics will constrain the available options for strategies, but the tactics should always flow from the strategy, and the strategy from the goal. Unfortunately, these days, people often seem to do it in reverse, enacting tactics out of a habitual response or marshalling tactics into a strategy without more than a vague appreciation of the goal.

The goal is the destination. It is the condition that denotes victory. Of course, there are proximate goals and ultimate goals. It may be most realistic to avoid a linear approach and picture the ultimate goal as a horizon, the farthest imaginable destination, which will change with time as once-distant waypoints become clear, new goals emerge, and a static or utopian state is never reached. For anarchists, who desire a world without coercive hierarchies, the ultimate goal today seems to be the abolition of an interlocking set of systems that include the state, capitalism, patriarchy, white supremacy, and ecocidal forms of civilization. This ultimate goal is very far away—so far away that many of us avoid thinking about it because we may find we do not believe it is possible. Focusing on the immediate realities is vital, but ignoring the destination ensures that we will never get there.

The strategy is the path, the game plan for achieving the goal. It is the coordinated symphony of moves that leads to the checkmate. Would-be revolutionaries in the US, and probably elsewhere, are most negligent when it comes to strategies. They have a rough idea of the goal, and are intensively involved with the tactics, but often entirely forgo the creation and implementation of a viable strategy. In one regard, nonviolent activists typically have a leg up on revolutionary activists, as they often have well-developed strategies in pursuit of short-term goals. The trade-off tends to be a total avoidance of intermediate and long-term goals, probably because the short-term goals and strategies of pacifists box them into dead ends that would be highly demoralizing if they were acknowledged.

Finally, we have tactics, which are the actions or types of actions that produce results. Ideally, these results have a compounded effect, building momentum or concentrating force along the lines laid out by the strategy. Letter writing is a tactic. Throwing a brick through a window is a tactic. It is frustrating that all the controversy over "violence" and "nonviolence" is simply bickering over tactics, when people have, for the most part, not even figured out whether our goals are compatible, and whether our strategies are complementary or counterproductive. In the face of genocide, extinction, imprisonment, and a legacy of millennia of domination and degradation, we backstab allies or forswear participation in the struggle over trivial matters like smashing windows or arming ourselves? It boils one's blood!

To return to our cool and reasoned analysis of these matters, it is worth noting that goals, strategies, and tactics correlate on a common plane, but the same thing could be viewed as a goal, a strategy, or a tactic depending on the scope of observation. There are multiple levels of magnitude, and the relationship among the elements of a particular chain of goal-strategy-tactics exists on each level. A short-term goal may be a long-term tactic. Suppose that in the next year, we want to set up a free clinic; that is our goal. We decide on an illegalist strategy (based on the assessment that we can force the local powers to concede some autonomy or that we can go under their radar and occupy preexisting bubbles of autonomy), and the tactics we choose from might include squatting a building, informal fundraising, and training ourselves in popular (nonprofessional) health care. Now suppose that in our lifetime, we want to overthrow the state. Our plan of attack might be to build a militant popular movement that is sustained by autonomous institutions that people identify with and struggle to protect from inevitable government repression. At this level, setting up free clinics is merely a tactic, one of many actions that build power along lines recommended by the strategy, which presumes to chart the course for reaching the goal of liberation from the state.

Having already criticized pacifists' tendency to unify on the basis of common tactics rather than mutual goals, I will leave aside the liberal, pro-establishment pacifists and charitably assume a rough similarity of goals between nonviolent and revolutionary activists. Let's pretend that we all want complete liberation. That leaves a difference of strategies and tactics. Clearly, the total pool of tactics available to nonviolent activists is inferior, as they can use only about half the options open to revolutionary activists. In terms of tactics, nonviolence is nothing but a severe limitation of the total options. For nonviolence to be more effective than revolutionary activism, the difference would have to be in the strategies, in a particular *arrangement* of tactics that achieves an unrivaled potency while avoiding all of the tactics that might be characterized as "violent."

The four major types of pacifist strategy are the morality play, the lobbying approach, the creation of alternatives, and generalized disobedience. The distinctions are arbitrary, and, in specific instances, pacifist strategies blend elements of two or more of these types. I will show that none of these strategies confer an advantage on nonviolent activists; in fact, all of them are weak and shortsighted.

The morality play seeks to create change by working on people's opinions. As such, this strategy misses the point entirely. Depending on the specific variation—educating or occupying the moral high ground—different tactics prove useful, though, as we shall see, they do not lead anywhere.

One incarnation of this strategy is to educate people, to disseminate information and propaganda, to change people's opinions and win people's support in a campaign. This could mean educating people about poverty and influencing them to oppose the closing of a homeless shelter, or it could mean educating people about the oppressions of government and influencing them to support anarchy. (It is important to note what is meant by "support" in these two examples: verbal and mental support. Education might influence people to donate money or join a protest, but it rarely encourages people to change their life priorities or take substantial risks.) The tactics used for this education strategy would include holding speeches and forums; distributing pamphlets and other informational texts; using alternative and corporate media to focus on and spread information about the issue; and holding protests and rallies to capture people's attention and open space for discussion of the issue. Most of us are familiar with these tactics, as this is a common strategy for achieving change. We are taught that information is the basis of democracy, and, without examining the true meaning of that statement, we think it means we can create change by circulating ideas supported by facts. The strategy can be mildly effective in achieving very minor and fleeting victories, but it runs into several fatal barriers that prevent serious headway in pursuit of any long-term goals.

The first barrier is elite control of a highly developed propaganda system that can decimate any competing propaganda system nonviolent activists might create. Pacifism can't even keep itself from being co-opted and watered down—how do pacifists expect to expand and recruit? Nonviolence focuses on changing hearts and minds, but it underestimates the culture industry and thought control by the media.

> The conscious and intelligent manipulation of the organized habits and opinions of the masses is an important element in democratic society. Those who manipulate this unseen mechanism of society constitute an invisible government which is the true ruling power of our country.[2]

The quote above, written in 1928, is from Edward Bernays's important book, *Propaganda*. Bernays was not some fringe conspiracy theorist; in fact, he was very much a part of the invisible government he describes.

> [Bernays's] clients included General Motors; United Fruit; Thomas Edison; Henry Ford; the US Departments of State, Health, and Commerce; Samuel Goldwyn; Eleanor Roosevelt; the American Tobacco Company; and Procter & Gamble. He directed public relations programs for every US president from Calvin Coolidge, in 1925, to Dwight Eisenhower in the late 1950s."[3]

Since then, the public relations industry that Bernays helped form has only grown.

Whether against a local grassroots campaign or the broader struggle for revolution, the propaganda machine can mobilize to counter, discredit, factionalize, or drown out any ideological threat. Consider the recent US invasion of Iraq. It should have been a model for the success of this strategy. The information was there—facts debunking the lies about weapons of mass destruction and the connection between Saddam Hussein and Al-Qaida were publicly available months before the invasion began. The people were there—protests prior to the invasion were immense, though the involvement of protest participants rarely went beyond the vocal and symbolic, as we would expect from an education strategy. Alternative media was there—enabled by the internet it reached an especially large number of Americans. Yet the majority of public opinion in the US (which is what an education strategy seeks to capture) did not turn against the war until the corporate media began regularly disclosing information about the falsity of reasons for going to war and, more importantly, the mounting costs of the occupation. And, in full accordance with its nature, the corporate media did not disclose this information until significant segments of the elite themselves began to oppose the war—not because the war was wrong or because they had been educated and enlightened, but because they realized it was becoming counterproductive to US interests and US power.[4] Even in such ideal circumstances, non-violent activists using an education strategy could not overcome the corporate media.

In what can best be described as a stupefying social environment, the endless repetition and near-total information control of the corporate media are much more potent than solid, well-researched arguments supported by facts. I hope that all pacifists understand that the corporate media is as much an agent of authority as is the police force or military.

In the face of this, many activists look to alternative media. While spreading and further radicalizing alternative media is an important task, it cannot be the backbone of a strategy. It is readily apparent that while alternative media can be an effective tool in certain circumstances, it cannot go toe to toe with the corporate media, primarily because of gross inequities of scale. Alternative media is kept in check by a number of coercive market and legal factors. Getting information to millions of people is expensive, and the sponsors do not exist who will fund revolutionary press en masse. The Catch-22 is that there will be no loyal readership to subscribe to and fund a truly mass radical media as long as the general population is indoctrinated away from radical news sources and sedated by a culture of complacency. Beyond market pressures exists the problem of government regulation and intervention. The airwaves are the domain of the state, which can and does shut down or undermine radical radio stations that manage to find funding.[5] Governments around the world—led, of course, by the US—have also made a habit of repressing radical websites, whether by imprisoning the webmaster on bogus charges or seizing equipment and shutting down servers on the pretext of some terrorism investigation.[6]

The second barrier in the way of educating people toward revolution is a structurally reinforced disparity in people's access to education. Most people are not currently able to analyze and synthesize information that challenges the integral mythologies on which their identities and worldviews are based. This is true across class lines. People from poor backgrounds are more likely to be undereducated, kept in a mental environment that discourages the development of their vocabularies and analytical skills. The overeducation of people from wealthy backgrounds turns them into trained monkeys; they are intensively trained to use analysis only to defend or improve the existing system, while being incurably skeptical and derisive toward revolutionary ideas or suggestions that the current system is rotten to the core.

Regardless of economic class, most people in the US will respond to radical information and analysis with syllogism, moralism, and polemics. They will be more susceptible to pundits arguing conventional wisdoms with familiar slogans than to people presenting challenging facts and analysis. Because of this, activists taking an educational approach tend to dumb down the message so that they too can take advantage of the power of clichés and platitudes. Examples include anti-war activists who declare that "peace is patriotic" because it would be too difficult to explain the problems with patriotism in the current semiological terrain (never mind dynamiting the terrain) and culture jammers trying to find radical "memes."[7]

A third barrier is a false assumption about the potency of ideas. The education approach seems to assume that revolutionary struggle is a contest of ideas, that there is something powerful in an idea whose time has come. At its base it is a morality play, and it ignores the fact that, especially in the US, a good many people on the side of authority know quite well what they are doing. Because of the hypocrisy of our times, people who benefit from patriarchy, white supremacy, capitalism, or imperialism (nearly the entire population of the Global North) like to justify their complicity with systems of domination and oppression with any number of altruistic lies. But a skilled debater will find that a majority of these people, when argued into a corner, will not have an epiphany—they will lash back with a primal defense of the evils that privilege them. Typically, white people will claim credit for the wonders of civilization and insist that their ingenuity entitles them to the benefits of legacies of slavery and genocide; wealthy people will claim that they have more right to own a factory or a hundred acres of real estate than a poor person has to food and shelter; men will joke about being the stronger sex and having a historically guaranteed right to rape; US citizens will belligerently assert that they have a right to other people's oil, or bananas, or labor, even after they can no longer obfuscate the nature of global economic relations. We forget that to maintain the current power structure, a good number of technicians, be they academics, corporate consultants, or government planners, have to constantly strategize to continue increasing their power and effectiveness. Democratic illusions can only run so deep, and, in the end, education will cause relatively few privileged people to truly support revolution. On certain levels, people with privilege already know what they are doing and what their interests are. Internal contradictions will emerge as the struggle gets closer to home, challenging the privileges on which their worldview and life experiences are based and threatening the possibility of a comfortable, enlightened revolution. People need more than education in order to commit to a painful and drawn-out struggle that will destroy the power structures that have encapsulated their very identities.

Education will not necessarily make people support revolution, and, even if it does, it will not build power. Contrary to the maxim of the information age, information is not power. Remember that *Scientia est potentia* (knowledge is power) is the watch phrase of those already at the helm of the state. Information itself is inert, but it guides the effective use of power; it has what military strategists would call a "force-multiplying effect." If we have a social movement with zero force to begin with, we can multiply that force however many times we wish and still have a big, fat zero. Good education can guide the efforts of an empowered social movement, just as useful information guides the strategies of governments, but the information itself will not change anything. Idly circulating subversive information in the current context only gives the government more opportunities to fine-tune its propaganda and its ruling strategies. People trying to educate their way to revolution are tossing gasoline onto a prairie fire and expecting that the right kind of fuel will stop the fire from burning them.

(On the other hand, education can be explosively effective when integrated into other strategies. In fact, many forms of education are necessary for building a militant movement and for changing the hierarchical social values that currently stand in the way of a free, cooperative world. Militant movements have to conduct a great deal of education to explain why they are forcefully struggling for revolution and why they have given up on legal means. But militant tactics open up possibilities for education that nonviolence can never tap. Because of its imperative principles, corporate media cannot ignore a bombing as easily as it can ignore a peaceful protest.[8] And even though the media will slander such actions, the more images of forceful resistance people receive through the media, the more the narcotic illusion of social peace is disrupted. People will begin to see that the system is unstable and change is actually possible, and, thus, overcome the greatest obstacle to change created by capitalist, media-driven democracies. Riots and insurrections are even more successful at creating ruptures in this dominant narrative of tranquility. Of course, much more than this is needed to educate people. In the end, we must destroy the corporate media and replace it with an entirely grassroots media. People who use a diversity of tactics can be much more effective at this, employing a number of innovative means to sabotage corporate newspapers and radio and television stations; hijack corporate media outlets and deliver an anti-capitalist broadcast; defend grassroots media outlets and punish the agencies responsible for repressing them; or expropriate money to fund and greatly increase the capacities of grassroots media outlets.[9])

Maintaining the moral high ground, which is a more overtly moralistic variation on this type of strategy, has a slightly different set of weaknesses but runs into the same dead end. In the short term, occupying the moral high ground can be effective, and it's easy to do when your opponents are white supremacist, chauvinistic, capitalist politicians. Activists can use protests, vigils, and various forms of denunciation and self-sacrifice to expose the immorality of government, either in particular or in general, and set themselves up as a righteous alternative. "Plowshares" anti-war activists often use this approach.

As a type of strategy for social change, occupying the moral high ground is weakened by the critical problem of obscurity, which is difficult to overcome given the same corporate-media barrier discussed above. And, in media-driven democracies, which turn the greater part of politics into a popularity contest, people are unlikely to see a miniscule, obscure group as either moral or imitable. However, the moral-high-ground approach sidesteps the challenge of educating a miseducated population by relying on extant moral values and simplifying revolutionary struggle to the zealous pursuit of a few principles.

A group that focuses on occupying the moral high ground also attracts potential recruits with something the corporate media cannot offer—an existential clarity and a sense of belonging. Plowshares pacifists and anti-war hunger strikers are often lifelong members. However, the corporate media is not the only institution for manufacturing social conformity. Churches, Elks lodges, and Boy Scout troops all occupy this niche as well, and, given the emphasis that morally elevated groups place on surrendering to in-group culture and values, there is little critical discourse or evaluation of the moralities involved; thus, having a morality that is more realistic or fair confers little actual advantage. What matters more is the elevation of a particular high ground, and these mainstream moral institutions are far stronger than pacifist groups in terms of access to resources—in other words, they are higher up and more visible in society, so they will overwhelmingly win the competition for new recruits. Due to the atomization and alienation of modern life, there are many gaps left unfilled by these moral institutions, and many lonely suburbanites still grasping for a sense of belonging, but radical pacifists will never be able to win more than a minority of these.

Those they do win will be more empowered than the members of a movement that aims simply to educate. People will go to great lengths to fight for a cause they believe in, to fight for a moral leader or ideal. But a moralistic movement has a greater potential than an education-based movement for empowering itself and becoming a dangerous thing (that is, eventually abandoning its pacifism). Woe to its allies, though. Such a movement will exhibit a mass authoritarianism and orthodoxy, and it will be particularly prone to factionalism. It will also be easily manipulated. There is perhaps no better example than Christianity, which evolved from opposition movement to potent weapon of the Roman Empire, from pacifistic cult to the most pathologically violent and authoritarian religion humanity has ever conceived.

In both variations of the morality-play approach to pacifist strategy, the purpose is to induce the majority of a society into joining or supporting a movement. (We can leave aside the laughable pretensions of simply enlightening or shaming the authorities into supporting revolution.) Both variations face terminal odds in pursuit of that majority due to the effective structural controls over culture within modern societies. In the unlikely chance that these odds were overcome, neither variation would be functionally capable of winning over more than a majority. Even if education were to become a more effective tool with privileged people it will not work against the elite and the enforcing class, who are given strong incentives and are culturally bound to the system, and occupying the moral high ground necessarily entails the creation of an inferior "other" to oppose.

At the absolute best, strategies of this type will lead to an oppositional but passive majority, which history has shown is easy for an armed minority to control (colonialism, for example). Such a majority could always switch to some other type of strategy that involves fighting and winning, but without any experience or even intellectual/moral familiarity with real resistance, the transition would be difficult. Meanwhile, the government would have recourse to easily exploitable flaws ingrained in the morality-play strategy, and an ostensibly revolutionary movement would have constrained itself to a horribly mismatched battle, trying to win hearts and minds without destroying the structures that have poisoned those hearts and minds.

Educating and building a liberating ethos are necessary to fully root out hierarchical social relationships, but there are concrete institutions such as law courts, public schools, boot camps, and public relations firms that are structurally immune to "changes of heart" and that automatically intervene in society to indoctrinate people in the morals that uphold hierarchical social relationships and capitalist production and consumption. Denying ourselves nonpacifist means to strengthen the movement and weaken or sabotage these structures leaves us in a sinking boat, with a little bucket to bail out the water pouring in through a ten-foot-wide hole, pretending we'll soon be high enough in the water to set sail toward our goal. This seems like waiting for pie in the sky, and it really should not qualify as a strategy. In a short-term battle to prevent a new coal mine or waste incinerator from coming into the neighborhood, it is possible to come up with a savvy media strategy within pacifist constraints (especially if your education campaign includes information about how the mine will harm privileged people in the area). But in pursuit of any lasting changes, strategies of this type usually can't even successfully lead to the dead end they inevitably create.

Would-be revolutionaries exemplify the ineffectiveness of nonviolence in building power when they approach their struggle as a morality play, and also when they take the lobbying approach. Lobbies were built into the political process by institutions that already had significant power (for example, corporations). Activists can build power by holding protests and demonstrating the existence of a constituency (on which their lobbyists bank), but this method for funneling power to lobbies is much weaker, pound for pound, than the cold, hard cash of corporations. Thus, "revolutionary" lobbies are impotent compared to opposing lobbies of the status quo. Lobbying also leads to a hierarchical and disempowered movement. The vast majority are simply sheep who sign petitions, raise funds, or hold protest signs, while an educated, well-dressed minority who seek audience with politicians and other elites hold all the power. Lobbyists will eventually identify more with the authorities than with their constituents—courting power, they fall in love with it, and betrayal becomes likely. If politicians run up against a morally upright, uncompromising lobbyist, they will simply deny that lobbyist an audience, pulling the rug out from under her organization. Activist lobbies are most successful when they are willing to compromise their constituency (representative politics in a democracy being the art of selling out a constituency while maintaining its loyalty). Some groups attempting to pressure the authorities do not appoint any specialized lobbyists, and thus avoid developing an elite leadership that will be co-opted by the system; however, they have still put themselves in the position of mobilizing pressure to get the system to change itself.

Nonviolent activists using the lobbying strategy attempt to craft a passive realpolitik to exercise leverage. But the only way to use leverage against the state in pursuit of interests diametrically opposed to those of the state is to threaten the state's existence. Only such a threat can make the state reconsider its other interests, because the state's primary interest is self-perpetuation. In his interpretive history of the Mexican revolution and land redistribution, John Tutino points out, "But only the most persistent and often violent rebels, like the Zapatistas, received land from the new leaders of Mexico. The lesson was clear: only those who threatened the regime got land; thus those seeking land must threaten the regime."[10] This was from a government supposedly allied with Mexico's agrarian revolutionaries—what do pacifists think they'll get from governments whose favored constituency is avowedly the corporate oligarchs? Frantz Fanon expressed the same sentiment in a similar way with regard to Algeria:

> When in 1956...the Front de Libération Nationale, in a famous leaflet, stated that colonialism only loosens its hold when the knife is at its throat, no Algerian really found these terms too violent. The leaflet only expressed what every Algerian felt at heart: colonialism is not a thinking machine, nor a body endowed with reasoning faculties. It is violence in its natural state, and it will only yield when confronted with greater violence.[11]

The lessons of Algeria and the Mexican revolution apply throughout history. The struggle against authority will be violent, because authority itself is violent and the inevitable repression is an escalation of that violence. Even "good government" will not redistribute power downward unless it is threatened with the loss of all its power. Lobbying for social change is a waste of scarce resources for radical movements. Imagine if all the millions of dollars and hundreds of thousands of volunteer hours from progressives and even radicals that went to lobby for some piece of legislation or to defeat the reelection of some politician instead went into funding activist social centers, free clinics, prisoner-support groups, community conflict-resolution centers, and free schools? We might actually lay the foundation for a serious revolutionary movement. Instead, a huge amount of effort is wasted.

Further, activists using the lobbying approach fail to see that making demands to authority is bad strategy. Nonviolent activists put all their energy into forcing authorities to hear their demands when they could use this energy to build power, to build a base from which to wage war. If they are successful, what will they have accomplished? At most, the government will mutter a brief apology, lose a little face, and meet the demand on paper (though, in reality, they'll just juggle things around to obscure the problem). After this, the activists will lose their momentum and initiative. They will have to go on the defensive, change directions, and readjust their campaign to point out that the reform is a fraudulent one. Their organization's disillusioned members will drop out, and the general public will perceive the organization as whiny and impossible to satisfy. (No wonder so many lobby-oriented activist organizations claim victory at the most hollow of compromises!)

Consider, for example, the School of the Americas Watch (SOAW). For more than a dozen years, the organization used annual passive protests, documentaries, and education campaigns to build lobbying power to convince politicians to support a bill to close the School of the Americas (SOA), an Army school that trained tens of thousands of Latin American officers and soldiers who were complicit in most of the worst human-rights abuses and atrocities in their respective countries. By 2001, SOAW almost had enough congressional support to pass a bill to shut down the SOA. Sensing the danger, the Pentagon simply introduced an alternative bill which "closed" the SOA while immediately reopening it under a different name. The politicians took the easy exit and passed the Pentagon bill. For years afterward, SOAW could not regain the support of many of the politicians, who claimed they wanted to wait and see if the "new" school was an improvement. If SOAW ever does succeed in closing the school by whatever name it calls itself, the military can simply spread out its torture-training operations to other military bases and programs throughout the country, or shift most of that work to military advisers abroad. If that happens, SOAW will be caught without a viable strategy, without having made any dent in US militarism.[12] When has the US government ever let a law or treaty stop it from doing what it wanted to do?

On the contrary, if radicals shifted their approach to directly fight US militarism, and if they could constitute a real threat without ever approaching a negotiating table, frightened government officials would begin drafting compromises and legislating reforms in an effort to prevent revolution. Decolonization, civil rights legislation, and nearly every other major reform was won in this manner. Radicals need never box themselves in or ensure betrayal by standing in a lobby or sitting down at the negotiating table. By refusing to be placated, revolutionaries drive a harder bargain than those whose aim is to bargain. Even when they lose, militant movements tend to cause reforms. The Red Brigades in Italy were ultimately unsuccessful, but they mounted such a threat that the Italian state instituted a number of far-reaching social-welfare and culturally progressive measures (for example, expanding public education and social spending, decentralizing some government functions, bringing the Communist Party into the government, and legalizing birth control and abortion) in an effort to drain support from the militants' base through reformism.[13]

The alternative-building approach employs one important component of a revolutionary strategy but underestimates all the complementary components that are necessary for success. The idea is that by creating alternative institutions, we can provide for an autonomous society and demonstrate that capitalism and the state are undesirable.[14] In actuality, while building these alternatives is of the utmost importance in creating and sustaining a revolutionary movement and laying the groundwork for the liberated societies that will come after revolution, it is absolutely absurd to think that the government will sit back and let us build science-fair experiments that will prove its obsolescence.

Events in Argentina surrounding the 2001 economic collapse (for example, the factory takeovers) have greatly inspired anti-authoritarians. Nonviolent anarchists (many of whom are academics) who favor the strategy of peacefully creating alternative institutions use a watered-down interpretation of events in Argentina to inject some life into their otherwise limp strategy. But the occupied factories in Argentina have survived by one of two means: either becoming legally recognized and recuperated into a capitalist economy, simply a more participatory form of corporation; or putting in their time at the barricades—fighting off police attempts to evict them with clubs and slingshots and building alliances with militant neighborhood assemblies so that the authorities fear a spreading of the conflict if they escalate their tactics. And the factory movement is on the defensive. Its practice and theory are in conflict because, in general, it is not headed toward a goal of replacing capitalism by spreading worker-controlled alternatives. The radical workers' major weakness has been an inability to expand their movement by the expropriation of factories where the managers are still in charge.[15] Such a course would put them in greater conflict with the state than they are currently ready for. To be sure, they are providing an important and inspiring example, but as long as they are only able to take over factories that have already been abandoned, they have not created a model for actually replacing capitalism.

At the 2004 North American Anarchist Convergence, keynote speaker Howard Ehrlich advised today's anarchists to act as though the revolution were already here and to build the world we want to see. Leaving aside the meaninglessness of this advice for people in prison, indigenous people faced with genocide, Iraqis trying to survive under occupation, Africans dying of diarrhea simply because they are deprived of clean water, and a majority of the world's other people, his statement makes me wonder how

Ehrlich could miss the lengthy history of government repression of autonomous spaces in service of revolutionary movements.

In Harrisonburg, Virginia, we set up an anarchist community center, allowed homeless people to sleep there through the winter, and provided free food and clothes out of that space. Within six months the cops shut us down using a creative array of zoning laws and building codes.[16] In the 1960s, the police took an active interest in sabotaging the Black Panther program that provided free breakfast to children.

How exactly are we supposed to build alternative institutions if we are powerless to protect them from repression? How will we find land on which to build alternative structures when everything in this society has an owner? And how can we forget that capitalism is not timeless, that once everything was an "alternative," and that the current paradigm developed and expanded precisely out of its ability to conquer and consume those alternatives?

Ehrlich is right that we need to start building alternative institutions now, but wrong to de-emphasize the important work of destroying existing institutions and defending ourselves and our autonomous spaces in the process. Even when mixed with more aggressive nonviolent methods, a strategy based on building alternatives that constrains itself to pacifism will never be strong enough to resist the zealous violence that capitalist societies employ when they conquer and absorb autonomous societies.

Finally, we have the nonviolent strategic approach of generalized disobedience. This tends to be the most permissive of nonviolent strategies, often condoning property destruction and symbolic physical resistance, although disciplined nonviolent campaigns of nonviolence and disobedience also fall within this type. The recent film *The Fourth World War*[17] is at the militant edge of this conception of revolution, highlighting resistance struggles from Palestine to Chiapas while conveniently hiding the significant segments of those movements engaged in armed struggle, probably for the comfort of US audiences. Disobedience strategies seek to shut the system down through strikes, blockades, boycotts, and other forms of disobedience and refusal. While many of these tactics are extremely useful when building toward a real revolutionary practice, the strategy itself has a number of gaping holes.

This type of strategy can only create pressure and leverage; it can never succeed in destroying power or delivering control of society to the people. When a population engages in generalized disobedience, the powerful face a crisis. The illusion of democracy is not working: this is a crisis. Highways have been blockaded, and business has been brought to a crawl: this is a crisis. But the people in power still control a large surplus; they are not in danger of being starved out by the strike. They control all the capital in the country, though some of this has been disabled by occupations and blockades. Most importantly, they still have control of the military and police (elites have learned much more about retaining the loyalty of the military since the Russian Revolution, and, in recent decades, the only significant military defections have occurred when the military faced violent resistance and the government seemed to be in its death throes; the police, for their part, have always been loyal lackeys). Behind closed doors, business leaders, government leaders, and military leaders confer. Perhaps they have not invited certain shamed members of the elite; perhaps multiple factions are scheming to come out of this crisis on top. They can use the military to break through any nonviolent barricade, retake any occupied factory, and seize the product of their labor if the rebels try to conduct an autonomous economy. Ultimately, the powerful can arrest, torture, and kill all the organizers; drive the movement underground; and restore order in the streets. A rebellious population that is conducting sit-ins or throwing rocks cannot stand up to a military that has been given free reign to use all the weapons in its arsenal. But behind closed doors, the country's leaders agree that such methods are not preferable; they are a last resort. Using them would destroy the illusion of democracy for years, and it would scare away investors and hurt the economy. So they win by letting the rebels declare victory: under pressure from business and military leaders, the president and a few other elected politicians step down (or, better yet, flee in a helicopter); the corporate media call it a revolution and begin trumpeting the populist credentials of the replacement president (who has been picked by the business and military leaders); and activists in the popular movement, if they have constrained themselves to nonviolence rather than preparing for the inevitable escalation of tactics, lose just when they are finally at the threshold of revolution.

In its long history, this strategy type has not succeeded in causing the class of owners, managers, and enforcers to defect and be disobedient, because their interests are fundamentally opposed to the interests of those who participate in the disobedience. What disobedience strategies have succeeded in doing, time and time again, is forcing out particular government regimes, though these are always replaced by other regimes constituted from among the elite (sometimes reformist moderates and sometimes the leadership of the opposition movement itself). This happened in India at the time of decolonization and in Argentina in 2001; with Marcos in the Philippines and with Milosevic in Serbia (this latter example, and similar "revolutions" in Georgia, Ukraine, and Lebanon, show the ineffectiveness of generalized disobedience in actually delivering social power to the people; all of these popular coups were actually orchestrated and financed by the US to install more market-friendly, pro-US politicians).[18] It is not even proper to say the old regimes are "forced out." Faced with rising disobedience and the threat of real revolution, they *choose* to hand over power to new regimes that they trust to honor the basic frameworks of capitalism and state. When they do not have the option of a transfer of power, they take off the gloves and attempt to brutalize and dominate the movement, which cannot defend itself and survive without escalating tactics. This is what happened to the anti-authoritarian labor movement in the US in the 1920s.

Generalized disobedience strategies attempt to shut down the system, and even in that endeavor they are less effective than militant strategies. Within the same context as that required for generalized disobedience—a broad and well-organized rebellious movement—if we do not restrict the movement to nonviolence, but support a diversity of tactics, it will be tremendously more effective. In terms of shutting the system down, there can be no comparison between peacefully locking down to a bridge or train line and blowing it up. The latter causes a longer-lasting obstruction, costs more to be cleared up, requires a more dramatic response from the authorities, does more to damage the morale and public image of the authorities, and allows the perpetrators to escape and fight another day. Blowing up a train line (or using some less dramatic and less threatening form of sabotage, if the social situation suggests that this will be more effective) will scare and anger people opposed to the liberation movement more than a peaceful lockdown will. But it will also cause them to take the movement more seriously, rather than dismiss it as a nuisance. (Of course, those who practice a diversity of tactics have the option to carry out a peaceful lockdown or an act of sabotage, depending on their estimation of what the public response will be.)

While somewhat useful to workers, a strategy of generalized disobedience has no relevance to already marginalized, surplus populations such as the many indigenous nations slated for expulsion or extermination, because their participation is not vital to the functioning of the aggressor state. The Aché of the Amazon do not pay any taxes to withhold, and they do not work any jobs to walk out from. The genocidal campaign against them does not hinge on their cooperation or noncooperation. People whom the authorities would love to see just up and die can win no leverage through disobedience.

As we have seen, the major types of nonviolent strategies all encounter insurmountable dead ends in the long term. Morality-play strategies misunderstand the way the state maintains control; thus, they are blind to the barriers posed by media and cultural institutions, and they offer no counter to the ability of armed minorities to control unarmed majorities. The lobbying approach wastes resources trying to pressure the government into acting in contradiction to its own interests. Strategies centered on building alternatives ignore the state's ability to repress radical projects and capitalism's talent for absorbing and corrupting autonomous societies. Generalized disobedience strategies open the door to revolution but deny popular movements the tactics necessary to expropriate direct control of the economy, redistribute wealth, and destroy the repressive apparatus of the state.

The long-term view that shows these nonviolent strategy types to be ineffective also makes the chances of any militant strategy seem bleak, seeing as how most anarchist communities in the US today are probably completely unprepared to defend themselves against the state. But it is in our everyday organizing that anti-authoritarians can strategically overcome passivity and foster militancy, and thus change the prospects for future struggles. Nonviolent strategies prevent this work. They also disadvantage us in interactions with the police and media, two examples that are worth going into.

Nonviolence plays into community policing and crowd control strategies. The tactics of pacifism, like many of the tactics of modern crowd control policing, are designed to de-escalate potentially insurrectionary situations. In his recent book detailing the history and development of the modern US police forces, *Our Enemies in Blue*, Kristian Williams documents how the crisis of the 1960s and 70s demonstrated to police that their methods of dealing with popular insurrection (such as urban riots and militant protests) only encouraged more resistance and more violence on the part of the resisters.[19] The resistance was empowered, the police lost control, and the government had to send in the military (further eroding the illusion of democracy and opening the possibility of real rebellion). In the years afterward, the police developed community policing strategies—to improve their image and control potentially subversive community organizing—and crowd control tactics emphasizing de-escalation. Descriptions of these tactics mirror exactly pacifist recommendations for conducting protests. The police allow minor forms of disobedience while maintaining communication with protest leaders, whom they pressure in advance to get the protest to police itself. "Peace marshals," police liaisons, and march permits are all aspects of this police strategy, which leads me to wonder if pacifists came up with these ideas independently, as a function of their implicitly statist mentality, or if they were so enthusiastic about loving their enemy that they swallowed whole the suggestions of that enemy for how to conduct the resistance. Either way, as long as we continue to tolerate nonviolent leadership, the police will have us right where they want us. But if we refuse to de-escalate and to cooperate with the police, we can organize disruptive protests when they are needed and fight for the interests of our community or our cause without compromise.

Nonviolence also leads to bad media strategies. Nonviolent codes of conduct for protest actions contradict the number-one rule of media relations: always stay on message. Nonviolent activists do not need to employ nonviolence codes to keep themselves peaceful. They do it to enforce ideological conformity and to assert their leadership over the rest of the crowd. They also do it as insurance, so that if any uncontrollable elements do act violently during a protest, they can protect their organization from being demonized in the media. They whip out the nonviolence code as proof that they were not responsible for the violence, and prostrate themselves before the reigning order. At this point, they have already lost the media war. The typical exchange goes something like this:

> Reporter: What do you have to say about the windows that were smashed in today's protest?

> Protestor: Our organization has a well-publicized nonviolence pledge. We condemn the actions of extremists who are ruining this protest for the well-meaning people who care about saving the forests/stopping the war/halting these evictions.

Activists rarely get more than two-line quotes or ten-second clips in the corporate media. The nonviolent activists exemplified in this skit waste their fleeting spotlight by going on the defensive; making their issue secondary to the concerns of the elite (property destruction by protestors); seemingly admitting weakness, failure, and disorganization to the public (by simultaneously taking responsibility for other protestors while bemoaning failure to control them); and, not least of all, backstabbing allies in public and dividing the movement.[20] That exchange should have looked like this:

> Reporter: What do you have to say about the windows that were smashed in today's protest?

> Protestor: It pales in comparison to the violence of deforestation/the war/these evictions. [Insert potent facts about the issue.]

If pressed, or asked by law enforcement, activists might insist that they were not personally responsible for the property destruction and cannot comment on the motivations of those who were. (But it is best not to talk with members of the corporate media as though they were human beings because they rarely comport themselves in such a manner. Activists should only answer in concise statements that tactfully address the issue; otherwise, editors are likely to run inane quotes and censor informative or challenging quotes.) If activists are successful in keeping the focus on the actual issue, they can avail themselves of subsequent opportunities to clear their names while again driving home the issue at hand (with tactics such as writing letters to the editor or protesting a media outlet's libelous accusations). But if activists are more concerned with clearing their names than addressing the issue, they are stillborn.

At first glance, a militant conception of revolution seems more impractical than a nonviolent conception, but this is because it is realistic. People need to understand that capitalism, the state, white supremacy, imperialism, and patriarchy all constitute a war against the people of this planet. And revolution is an intensification of that war. We cannot liberate ourselves and create the worlds we want to live in if we think of fundamental social change as shining a light in the darkness, winning hearts and minds, speaking truth to power, bearing witness, capturing people's attention, or any other passive parade. Millions of people die every year on this planet for no better reason than a lack of clean drinking water. Because the governments and corporations that have usurped control of the commons have not found a way to profit from those people's lives, they let them die. Millions of people die every year because a few corporations and their allied governments do not want to allow the production of generic AIDS drugs and other medicine. Do you think the institutions and the elite individuals who hold the power of life or death over millions give a fuck about our protests? They have declared war on us, and we need to take it back to them. Not because we are angry (though we should be), not to get revenge, and not because we are acting impulsively, but because we have weighed the possibility of freedom against the certainty of shame from living under whatever form of domination we are faced with in our particular corner of the globe; because we realize that some people are already fighting, often alone, for their liberation, and that they have a right to and we should support them; and because we understand that the overlapping prisons that entomb our world have by now been so cleverly constructed that the only way to free ourselves is to fight and destroy these prisons and defeat the jailers by whatever means necessary.

Realizing that this is a war can help us decide what we need to do and craft effective strategies for the long haul. Those of us living in North America, Europe, and some other parts of the world live under the illusion of democracy. The government politely pretends it would never kill us if we challenged its authority, but that is a thin veneer. In his annual address to Congress, on December 3, 1901, President Theodore Roosevelt, speaking of the enemy of the day, declared: "We should war with relentless efficiency not only against anarchists, but against all active and passive sympathizers with anarchists."[21] One hundred years later, in September 2001, President George W. Bush announced: "Either you are with us, or you are with the terrorists."[22]

Aside from showing how little our government has changed in a century, this quote poses an interesting question. Of course we can reject Bush's demand that if we do not line up with Osama bin Laden then we should declare allegiance to the White House. But if we insist on disloyalty, then regardless of our personal affiliations Bush has judged us as terrorists, and the Justice Department has demonstrated that it might prosecute us as such—in its campaign against the radical environmental activists it has labeled "ecoterrorists";[23] in the Joint Terrorism Task Force's spying on dissidents; and in the harassment, repression, and deportation of Muslims and immigrants that has been the major domestic "security" activity of the government since September 11. We could proudly recognize that "terrorist" has been governments' label of choice for freedom fighters for decades, and certainly this honor is premature given the state of our movement. But the pacified resistance in the US is not comfortable in the role of freedom fighter. Instead of acknowledging the war that already exists, we have shuffled over to the safe side of Bush's dichotomy, whether we admit it or not, and nonviolence has been our excuse.

General Frank Kitson, an influential British military, police, and social-control theoretician whose strategies have been disseminated and adopted by state planners and police agencies in the US, breaks social disturbances down into three stages: preparation, nonviolence, and insurgency.[24] Police understand this, and they do what they can to keep dissidents and disaffected masses held back in the first two stages. Many of those dissidents do not understand this. They do not understand what it will take to redistribute power in our society, and they prevent themselves and their allies from going all the way.

Quite evidently, the state is more afraid of militant groups than nonviolent groups, and I have used this as evidence that militant groups are more effective. The state understands that it has to react more forcefully and energetically to neutralize militant revolutionary movements. I have heard quite a few nonviolent activists turn this very fact on its head to argue that nonviolent attempts at revolution are more effective because militant attempts will be savagely repressed (and in other chapters I have quoted these activists to show that their primary concern is their own safety). True, the path to revolution envisioned by militant activists is much more dangerous and difficult than the one envisioned by pacifists, but it also has the advantage of being realistic, unlike the pacifist fantasy. But this logical juggling is worth examining.

Pacifists claim they are more effective because they are more likely to survive repression. The reasoning is that militants give the state an excuse to eliminate them (the excuse being self-defense against a violent enemy), whereas states are unable to use overwhelming violence against pacifists because there can be no justification. The gullible assumption on which this reasoning is based is that governments are ruled by public opinion, rather than vice versa. Getting past the sophistry of nonviolence, we can easily establish the factor that determines whether government repression will be a popular measure in the court of public opinion. That factor is the popular legitimacy, or lack thereof, which the resistance movement enjoys—it has nothing to do with violence or nonviolence. If the people do not see a resistance movement as legitimate or important, if they wave the flag with all the rest, they will cheer even when the government carries out massacres. But if the people sympathize with the resistance movement, then government repression will foster more resistance. The slaughter of a peaceful group of Cheyenne and Arapaho at Sand Creek only brought applause from the white citizenry of the Union; similar was the national response to the repression of harmless "communists" in the 1950s. But at times of peak popularity, British attempts to repress the Irish Republican Army (IRA) only brought more support for the IRA and more shame to the Brits, both within Ireland and internationally. In the last decade, Serbian attempts to crush the Kosovo Liberation Army had the same effect.

The government is able to repress both nonviolent and militant groups without causing a backlash so long as it has control over the ideological terrain. Nonviolent groups can operate with less cultural independence and popular support because they tend to aim lower and pose less of a threat, whereas a militant group, by its very existence, is a direct challenge to the state monopoly on force. Militant groups understand that they need to overcome the state, and, until they help create a broad culture of resistance (or unless they arise out of such a culture), they will be isolated and on the run. Pacifists, on the other hand, have the option of forswearing confrontation with state power and pretending they are engaged in some process of magically transforming the state through the "power of love," or their "nonviolent witness," or by disseminating heartwrenching images of cardboard puppets through the media, or some other swill. The prevalence or scarcity of pacifism is a good barometer for the weakness of the movement. Strong popular support allows a radical movement to survive repression; if a movement has built popular support for militant struggle against the state, they are that much closer to victory.

A state decides to repress activists and social movements when it perceives dissidents' goals as threatening and achievable. If the goal is to seize or destroy state power, and agents of the state think there is any chance of approaching that goal, they will repress or destroy the movement, regardless of the tactics advocated. Does violence encourage repression? Not necessarily. Let us consider some case studies and compare the repression of the Wobblies with that of the immigrant Italian anarchists or the Appalachian miners. All three cases took place in the same time period, through World War I and the 1920s, in the United States.

The Industrial Workers of the World (IWW)—members were known as "Wobblies"—was an anarchist labor union seeking the abolition of wage labor. At its peak in 1923, the IWW had nearly half a million members and active supporters. In the earlier days, the union was militant: some of the IWW leaders encouraged sabotage. However, the union never fully rejected nonviolence, and its main tactics were education, protest, "free speech fights," and civil disobedience. The IWW's above-ground organization and centralized structure made it an easy target for government repression. In response to state pressure, the organization did not even take a position to oppose World War I. "In the end, the leadership decided against explicitly encouraging the membership to violate the law [by opposing the draft]. The way they were subsequently treated by federal and state officials, however, they may as well have."[25] The Wobblies also accommodated state demands for passivity by suppressing a pamphlet of a 1913 Elizabeth Gurley Flynn speech encouraging sabotage. The IWW withdrew similar books and pamphlets from circulation and "officially renounced the use of sabotage by any of its members."[26] Of course, none of these actions saved the union from repression because the government had already identified it as a threat to be neutralized. The IWW's goal (abolition of wage labor through the gradual shortening of the work week) was a threat to the capitalist order, and the size of the union gave it the power to circulate these dangerous ideas and carry out significant strikes. One hundred Chicago Wobblies were put on trial in 1918, in addition to IWW organizers from Sacramento and Wichita; the government accused them of sedition, advocating violence, and criminal syndicalism. All were convicted. After the imprisonment and other repression (including lynchings of IWW organizers in some cities), "the dynamic force of the union was lost; it never regained its hold on the American labor movement."[27] The Wobblies accommodated state power and pacified themselves, renouncing violent tactics; this was a step along the road of their repression. They were jailed, beaten, lynched.

The government repressed them because of the radicalism and
popularity of their vision. Renouncing violence prevented them
from defending that vision.

Immigrant Italian anarchist militants living in New England
survived government repression at least as well as the Wobblies,
though their ranks were much smaller and their tactics more spectacular—they bombed the homes and offices of several government
officials, and they almost killed US attorney general A. Mitchell
Palmer.[28] The most militant of the Italian anarchists were the
Galleanists,[29] who threw themselves into the class war. Unlike the
Wobblies, they vocally and openly organized against World War
I, holding protests, making speeches, and publishing some of the
most uncompromising and revolutionary anti-war tracts in papers
such as *Cronaca Sovversiva* (which the Justice Department declared
"the most dangerous newspaper published in this country").[30] In
fact, several of them were shot to death by police at anti-war protests. The Galleanists energetically supported labor organizing in
New England factories and were key supporters of several major
strikes; they also found time to organize against the rising tide of
fascism in the US. But the Galleanists left their deepest mark with
their refusal to accept government repression.

They carried out dozens of bombings in New England cities
and in Milwaukee, New York, Pittsburgh, Philadelphia, DC, and
elsewhere, mostly in response to the arrest or killing of comrades
by state forces. Some of these attacks were well-coordinated campaigns involving multiple simultaneous bombings. The largest
was the 1920 bombing of Wall Street in response to the frame-up
of Sacco and Vanzetti (who were not involved in the Braintree
robbery for which they were executed but probably played support roles in some of the Galleanist bombings). That act killed
33 people, caused $2 million in damage, and destroyed, among
other things, the House of Morgan, J.P. Morgan's capitol building of American finance, as it were. The feds organized a massive
investigation and manhunt but never caught anybody. Paul Avrich

has established the bombing to be the work of a lone Galleanist, Mario Buda, who escaped to Italy and continued his work until he was arrested by the Mussolini regime.[31]

The government undertook major efforts to repress the Italian anarchists, and with only partial success. Government forces killed a few by police action or judicial execution, and imprisoned more than a dozen more, but unlike the Wobblies, the Galleanists avoided being arrested en masse. This was, in part, due to the decentralized, security-conscious forms of organization that the Italians' concept of militant revolution influenced them to adopt. And it should be noted that the Galleanists were especially at risk of government repression because, unlike many of the Wobblies, they could be targeted with WASP xenophobia and threatened with deportation. (In fact, about 80 of them were deported, yet the others were able to stay highly active.[32]) The Galleanists' uncompromising response to state repression had at least some measurable results in discouraging repression (aside from making both government and factory bosses afraid to do anything to further incite their workers, lest they join the anarchist bomb throwers). Through the threat of letter bombs, they caused the prodigal Bureau of Investigation detective who had been instrumental in tracking down and arresting several of their comrades in 1918 to go into hiding and then leave the bureau entirely in 1919.[33] The only consequences that the government agents responsible for repressing the Wobblies had to deal with were promotions.

From 1919 to 1920, the height of the Red Scare took its toll on the Italian anarchists, though they remained active and uncompromising and did not fold as quickly as the Wobblies. In October 1920, *Cronaca Sovversiva*, the newspaper that served as a hub for many of the Galleanists, was finally suppressed by the authorities, and the focus of immigrant Italian anarchist activity returned to Italy, to which many of the activists fled or were deported. The end of their movement in the United States was not the end of their movement overall, however, and for several years these anarchists were key opponents to Mussolini, who, like his American colleagues, feared them and prioritized their repression. (In fact, the new Bureau of Investigation director, J. Edgar Hoover, supplied the fascists with invaluable information for the specific purpose of destroying the Italian anarchists.[34]) And some of the exiled Italian anarchists took part in the Spanish Civil War in 1936. Though Italian anarchism in the US "never recovered" after 1920, "the anarchists by no means vanished from the scene."[35] With an international focus, they organized opposition to the rising communist and fascist dictatorships (they were at the "forefront of antifascist struggle" in Little Italys throughout the US),[36] and also turned Sacco and Vanzetti's support campaign into a worldwide cause.

Far from being universally alienating figures, Sacco and Vanzetti won the support of their communities—Italians as well as WASPs—and the support of public figures in the US and Europe, this despite being imprisoned and their continued call for violent revolution and bombing campaigns against the authorities. Their supporters on the outside did not disappoint them. From 1926 to 1932, anarchists carried out several more bombings, targeting the judge, the governor, the executioner, and the person whose call to the police got the two arrested; none of the bombers were ever caught. The Italian anarchists also continued to agitate and spread their ideas—the successor to *Cronaca Sovversiva*, *L'Adunata dei Refrattari*, was published for another 40 years, into the 1960s.

The 1921 Mine War in West Virginia offers another example of government responses to militant tactics. When the mine owners repressed the efforts of the miners to form unions—firing union members and bringing in scabs—Appalachian rebels responded forcefully. They opened fire on scabs and killed several coal-company thugs and deputies sent to repress them. In time, a guerrilla conflict and then a full-blown war developed. On several occasions, police and company thugs opened fire on miners' encampments, targeting women and children. In the most famous massacre, they gunned down Sid Hatfield, who, in his capacity as sheriff, actually fought against the repression carried out by company thugs. Thousands of armed miners formed an army and marched on Logan, West Virginia, to remove (and hang) the sheriff there, who was especially active in repressing the union miners. The US Army responded with thousands of troops, machine guns, and even bombardment by airplanes in what became known as the Battle of Blair Mountain. After the battle, the union miners backed down. But despite participating in one of the century's largest acts of armed mutiny, very few of them got serious prison sentences—most of the rebels received no punishment at all—and the government eased off somewhat and allowed the unionization of the mines (their union still exists today).[37]

More recently, police strategists writing about the anarchist movement have noted, "Intelligence gathering among the most radical—and often most violent—factions is particularly difficult....The very nature of the movement's suspicion and operational security enhancements makes infiltration difficult and time consuming."[38] So the claims that nonviolent groups are more likely to survive repression do not stand up to scrutiny. Excluding the tendency of pacifists to roll over in advance so they never pose a threat of changing anything, it seems that actually the opposite is true.

Consider a few timely points regarding nonviolent so-called resistance to the US occupation of Iraq, one of the most pressing issues of the day. Pacifism sees victory as avoiding or decreasing violence, so naturally pacifists cannot confront violence directly. Any real resistance to military occupation would lead to an increase in violence (as the occupiers attempt to stamp out resistance) before liberation and the possibility of real peace—it has to get worse before it gets better. If the Iraqi resistance is overcome, the situation will appear more peaceful, but, in reality, the spectacular violence of warfare will have turned into the threatened, invisible, and mundane violence of successful occupation, and the Iraqi people will be much further away from liberation. Yet nonviolent activists are prone to misinterpret this apparent peace as a victory, much as they interpreted the withdrawal of US troops from Vietnam as a victory, even though bombing intensified and a US-backed regime continued to occupy South Vietnam.

What nonviolent anti-war activists are unable to realize is that the most important resistance, probably the only significant resistance, to the occupation of Iraq is the resistance being waged by the Iraqi people themselves. On the whole, the Iraqis have chosen armed struggle.[39] Americans who condemn this while lacking any personal knowledge of what it is like to organize resistance in Iraq only flaunt their ignorance. People in the US who claim to be anti-war use nonviolence as an excuse to avoid their responsibility to support the Iraqi resistance. They also parrot corporate media propaganda and pretend that all Iraqi resistance groups are composed of authoritarian, patriarchal fundamentalists, when it is an accessible fact, to anyone who cares to know, that the Iraqi resistance contains a great diversity of groups and ideologies. Nonviolence, in this case, is a greater obstacle than the fear of government repression to building relationships of solidarity and becoming critical allies to the most liberatory of resistance groups. Condemning them all ensures that the only groups getting outside support are the authoritarian, patriarchal, fundamentalist ones. The approach of the US anti-war movement in relation to the Iraqi resistance does not merely qualify as bad strategy: it reveals a total lack of strategy, and it is something we need to fix.

The strategies of nonviolence cannot defeat the state—they tend to reflect a lack of understanding of the very nature of the state. The power of the state is self-perpetuating; it will defeat liberation movements with any means at its disposal. If attempts to overthrow such a power structure survive the first stages of repression, the elite will turn the conflict into a military one, and people using nonviolent tactics cannot defeat a military. Pacifism cannot defend itself against uncompromising extermination. As explained in one study of revolution in modern societies:

> During World War II the Germans were not familiar with passive resistance (when it occurred); but today's armed forces

are far better prepared to cope with non-violence, both techni-cally and psychologically. Advocates of non-violence, one Brit-ish military specialist reminds us, "are inclined to overlook that fact that its main successes have been obtained against opponents whose code of morality was fundamentally simi-lar, and whose ruthlessness was thereby restrained...The only impression it seems to have made on Hitler was to excite his impulse to trample on what, to his mind, was contemptible weakness...." If we accept the premise of the black revolution-ists in this country, namely, that we live in a racist society, less ruthlessness can hardly be expected....

It might be interesting to try to depict the course of a non-violent insurrection....Actually, "role-playing" experiments in "civilian defense" have already taken place. In a thirty-one hour experiment on Grindstone Island in Ontario Province, Canada, in August 1965, thirty-one non-violent "defenders" had to deal with six "armed" men representing a United States–supported "right wing Canadian government [which had] occupied major portions of the Canadian heartland..." At the end of the experiment, thirteen of the defenders were "dead"; the participants "concluded that the experiment had been a defeat for non-violence."[40]

The history of its practice leads me to the same conclusion: nonviolence cannot defend itself against the state, much less over-throw it. The proclaimed power of nonviolence is a delusion that gives its practitioners safety and moral capital to make up for an inability to win.

Ward Churchill has argued that pacifism is pathological. I would say that, at the least, the advancement of nonviolence as a revolutionary practice in the present context is dependent on a number of delusions. Where to begin?

Often, after showing that the victories of nonviolence were not victories at all, except for the state, I have encountered the simplistic counterargument that because some particular militant struggle or act of violence was unsuccessful, "violence" is equally ineffective. I don't recall ever hearing anyone say that the use of violence ensures victory. I hope everyone can see the difference between showing the failures of pacifist victories and showing the failures of militant struggles that no one ever claimed as victories. It is not controversial to assert that militant social movements have succeeded in changing society, or even becoming the prevalent force in society. To restate that: everyone must admit that struggles using a diversity of tactics (including armed struggle) can succeed. History is full of examples: revolutions in North and South America, France, Ireland, China, Cuba, Algeria, Vietnam, and so forth. It is also not terribly controversial to assert that anti-authoritarian militant movements have succeeded for a time in liberating areas and creating positive social changes in those areas. Cases in point include collectivization in the Spanish Civil War and in Makhno's Ukraine, the autonomous zone in the Shinmin Province created by the Korean Anarchist Communist Federation, and the temporary breathing room won for the Lakota by Crazy Horse and his warriors. What is debatable, to some, is whether militant movements can win and survive in the long term while remaining anti-authoritarian. To convincingly argue against this possibility, pacifists would have to show that

6

NONVIOLENCE IS DELUDED

using violence against an authority *inevitably* makes one take on authoritarian characteristics. This is something that pacifists have not done and cannot do.

Often, pacifists prefer to characterize themselves as righteous than to logically defend their position. Most people who have heard the arguments of nonviolence have witnessed the formulation or assumption that nonviolence is the path of the dedicated and disciplined, and that violence is the "easy way out," a giving in to base emotions.[1] This is patently absurd. Nonviolence is the easy way out. People who choose to commit themselves to nonviolence face a far more comfortable future than those who choose to commit themselves to revolution. A prisoner of the black liberation movement told me in correspondence that when he joined the struggle (as a teenager, no less), he knew he would end up either dead or in prison. Many of his comrades are dead. For continuing the struggle behind prison walls, he has been locked up in solitary confinement for longer than I have been alive. Compare this with the recent comfortable, commemorated deaths of David Dellinger and Phil Berrigan. Nonviolent activists can give their lives to their cause, and a few have, but, unlike militant activists, they do not face a point of no return after which there is no going back to a comfortable life. They can always save themselves by compromising their total opposition, and most do.

Aside from reflecting an ignorance of the reality of the different consequences of certain political actions, the belief that nonpacifist struggle is the easy way out is often tinged with racism. The authors of the essay "Why Nonviolence?" do their best throughout the entire essay to avoid mention of race, but in the question-and-answer section they provide a veiled response to criticisms that pacifism is racist by painting "oppressed people" (black people) as angry and impulse-driven. "Q: Demanding nonviolent behavior from oppressed people toward their oppressors is senseless and unfair! They need to act out their anger!"[2] The authors' "answer" to this contrived criticism of nonviolence includes many of the typical and deluded fallacies already discussed: the authors counsel people who are far more oppressed than they are to have patience with conditions they couldn't possibly comprehend; the authors advise people of color to act in a way that is "ennobling and pragmatic"; the authors forestall criticisms of racism by dropping the name of a token person of color; and the authors conclude by tacitly threatening that militant activism on the part of people of color will result in abandonment and betrayal by powerful white "allies." To wit:

> As for unfairness, if the oppressed could wish it away, they would no longer be oppressed. There is no pain-free road to liberation. Given the inevitability of suffering, it is both ennobling and pragmatic to present nonviolent discipline and suffering (as did Martin Luther King, Jr.) as imperatives. "Acting out anger" in a way that costs a group allies is a luxury serious movements cannot afford.[3]

Pacifists delude themselves in thinking of revolutionary activism as being impulsive, irrational, and coming solely from "anger." In fact, revolutionary activism, in some of its manifestations, has a pronounced intellectual streak. After the Detroit riots of 1967, a *government* commission found that the typical rioter (in addition to being proud of his or her race and hostile to white people and middle-class black people) "is substantially better informed about politics than Negroes who were not involved in the riots."[4] George Jackson educated himself in prison, and emphasized in his writings the need for militant black people to study their historical relationship to their oppressors and learn the "scientific principles" of urban guerrilla warfare.[5] The Panthers read Mao, Kwame Nkrumah, and Frantz Fanon, and required new members to educate themselves on the political theories behind their revolution.[6] When he was finally captured and brought to trial, revolutionary New Afrikan anarchist Kuwasi Balagoon rejected the court's legitimacy and proclaimed the right of black people to liberate themselves in a statement many pacifists could learn volumes from:

Before becoming a clandestine revolutionary i was a tenant organizer and was arrested for menacing a 270 pound colonial building superintendent with a machete, who physically stopped the delivery of oil to a building i didn't live in, but had helped to organize. Being an organizer for the Community Council on Housing i took part in not only organizing rent strikes, but pressed slumlords to make repairs and maintain heat and hot water, killed rats, represented tenants in court, stopped illegal evictions, faced off City Marshals, helped turn rents into repair resources and collective ownership by tenants and demonstrated whenever the needs of tenants were at stake....Then i began to realize that with all this effort, we couldn't put a dent in the problem...

Legal rituals have no effect on the historic process of armed struggle by oppressed nations. The war will continue and intensify, and as for me, i'd rather be in jail or in the grave than do anything other than fight the oppressor of my people. The New Afrikan Nation as well as the Native American Nations are colonialized within the present confines of the United States, as the Puerto Rican and Mexicano Nations are colonialized within as well as outside the present confines of the United States. We have a right to resist, to expropriate money and arms, to kill the enemy of our people, to bomb and do whatever else aids us in winning, and we will win.[7]

In comparison, the strategic and tactical analysis of nonviolent activism is rather simplistic, rarely rising above the regurgitation of hackneyed clichés and moralistic truisms. The amount of studious preparations required to successfully carry out militant actions, compared with the amount required for nonviolent actions, also contradicts the perception that revolutionary activism is impulsive.

People willing to acknowledge the violence of revolution—it is misleading to talk about choosing violence because violence is inherent in social revolution and the oppressive status quo that precedes it, whether we use violent means or not—are more likely to understand the sacrifices involved. Any knowledge of what revolutionaries prepare themselves for and go through demonstrates the cruelly ignorant farce of the pacifist proclamation that revolutionary violence is impulsive. As already mentioned, the writings of Frantz Fanon were among the most influential for black revolutionaries in the United States during the black liberation movement. The last chapter of his book *The Wretched of the Earth* deals entirely with "colonial war and mental disorders," with the psychological trauma incurred as a matter of course from colonialism and the "total war" waged by the French against the Algerian freedom fighters[8] (a war, I should note, that makes up a large part of the textbook used by the US in counterinsurgency warfare and wars of occupation up to the present moment). People who fight for revolution do know what they are getting into, to the extent that the horror of these things can be known. But do pacifists?

A further delusion (expressed by pacifists who want to appear militant and powerful) is that pacifists do fight back, only nonviolently. This is rubbish. Sitting down and locking arms is not fighting, it is a recalcitrant capitulation.[9] In a situation involving a bully or a centralized power apparatus, physically fighting back discourages future attacks because it raises the costs of oppression incurred by the oppressor. The meek resistance of nonviolence only makes it easier for the attacks to continue. At the next protest, for instance, see how reluctant the police are to fence in militant groups such as the black bloc and subject them all to mass arrest.[10] The cops know that they'll need one or two cops for every protestor and that some of them are going to end up badly hurt. The peaceful, on the other hand, can be barricaded in by a relatively small number of cops, who can then go into the crowd at their leisure and carry off the limp protestors one by one.

Palestine is another example. There can be no doubt that the Palestinians are an inconvenience to the Israeli state, and that the Israeli state has no concern for the well-being of the Palestinians.

If the Palestinians hadn't made the Israeli occupation and every successive aggression so costly, all the Palestinian land would be seized, except for a few reservations to hold the necessary number of surplus laborers to supplement the Israeli economy, and the Palestinians would be a distant memory in a long line of extinct peoples. Palestinian resistance, including suicide bombings, has helped ensure Palestinian survival against a far more powerful enemy.

Nonviolence further deludes itself and its converts with the truism "Society has always been violent. It is nonviolence that is revolutionary."[11] In practice, our society honors and commemorates both pro-state violence and respectable, dissident pacifism. The very activist who claimed that our society is already pro-violence can drop the name of Leon Czolgosz (the anarchist who assassinated President McKinley) in a guest op-ed in the local corporate newspaper and know that a mainstream audience will respond to that violent personage with condemnation. Meanwhile, the same activist references pacifists like King and Gandhi to give his beliefs an aura of respectability in the mainstream eye.[12] If society is already in favor of violence across the board, and pacifism is revolutionary enough to fundamentally challenge our society and its ingrained oppressions, why does Czolgosz warrant hatred while Gandhi warrants approval?

Pacifists also harbor delusions about the decency of the state and, subconsciously, about the amount of protection their privileges will afford them. Students leading the occupation of Tiananmen Square in "Autonomous Beijing" thought that their "revolutionary" government would not open fire on them if they remained a peaceful, loyal opposition. "The students' nearly complete misunderstanding of the nature of legitimacy under bureaucratic power and the illusion that the Party could be negotiated with, left them defenseless both in terms of the theoretical means of describing their undertaking and in regards to the narrow practice of civil disobedience it led them to adopt."[13] Thus, when the students who had put themselves in control of the movement refused to arm themselves (unlike many in the working-class suburbs, who were less educated and more intelligent), the whole movement was vulnerable, and Autonomous Beijing was crushed by the tanks of the People's Liberation Army. The students at Kent State were similarly shocked, even as the same government that killed a paltry number of them was massacring millions of people in Indochina without consequence or hesitation.

In the end, nonviolence has all the intellectual depth of a media sound bite. Pacifism requires a very vague, broad, loaded, and non-analytical term—*violence*—to take on a scientific precision. After all, not racism, not sexism, not homophobia, not authoritarianism, but violence, must be the critical axis of our actions. *Why would we take pledges of anti-racism before a march, or make participation in a movement contingent on being respectful of women, queer people, and trans people, when we can take far less divisive pledges of nonviolence?* The likelihood that most supporters of nonviolence codes have never even asked this question goes a long way toward demonstrating the limitation of pacifist thinking. So pacifists ignore real divisions such as white privilege and instead make baseless and potentially racist/classist distinctions between cutting a lock during a pre-announced demonstration so that protestors can conduct a die-in on a military base and smashing a window under cover of a riot so that a ghetto dweller can get food and money to take care of her family. Significantly, pacifists do not make the critical distinction between the structural, institutional, and systemically permitted personal violence of the state (the state being understood in a broad sense to include the functions of the economy and patriarchy) and the individualized social violence of the "criminal" sort or collective social violence of the "revolutionary" sort, aimed at destroying the far greater violence of the state. Pretending that all violence is the same is very convenient for supposedly anti-violence privileged people who benefit from the violence of the state and have much to lose from the violence of revolution.

Sneaking onto a military base, pouring one's blood on things, and hammering missiles, we are told, is nonviolent, but blowing up the Litton Systems plant (where cruise missile components were made) would have been violent even if no one had been injured. Why? The usual response is either that a bomb threatens people, whereas old white nuns with hammers do not, or that when activists use a bomb, they cannot ensure that people will not get hurt. The first argument ignores two facts: what is considered threatening is largely determined by preexisting prejudices against certain races and classes, and to the majority of the world's population outside North America, a nonfunctioning missile is far less threatening than a functioning missile, no matter how many bombs had to blow up in the Global North to achieve that end. There is certainly no doubt that bombing can destroy missiles better than hammering. The second argument, as I have noted, ignores the possibility of victims outside of North America. A bomb ensures that a factory will not be able to produce missiles far better than a hammer does, and missiles in the possession of imperialist states kill far more people than bombs (or hammers) in the possession of urban guerrilla groups. But this consideration is so far from the minds of pacifists that the nuns to whom I allude based much of their trial defense on the contention that they had not caused any real damage, only symbolic damage, to the missile facility they had infiltrated.[14] Can they even truly be considered nonviolent, after deliberately wasting an opportunity to decommission a major instrument of warfare?

At a workshop I gave on the flaws of nonviolence, I conducted a little exercise to demonstrate how vague this idea of violence actually is. I asked the participants, who included supporters of nonviolence and supporters of a diversity of tactics, to stand up and, as I slowly read a list of various actions, to walk to one spot if they considered the action violent, and to another spot if they considered the action nonviolent. The actions included such things as buying clothes made in a sweatshop, eating meat, a wolf killing a deer, killing someone who is about to detonate a bomb in a crowd, and so on. Almost never was there perfect agreement among the participants, and several of the actions that they considered violent they also considered moral, while some also considered certain nonviolent actions to be immoral. The concluding lesson of the exercise: Does it really make sense to base so much of our strategy, our alliances, and our involvement in activism on a concept that is so blurry that no two people can really agree on what it means?

Efforts to actually define *violence* lead to two outcomes. Either *violence* is defined literally as something that causes pain or fear, and it cannot be considered an immoral thing because it includes natural activities such as giving birth or eating other living beings to stay alive, or violence is defined with a moral concern for outcomes, in which case inaction or being ineffective in the face of a greater violence must also be considered violent.[15] Either definition excludes nonviolence—the first because violence is inevitable and normal, and the second because nonviolence must be considered violent if it fails to end a system of violence, and also because all privileged people must be considered complicit in violence whether or not they consider themselves pacifists. But pacifists still delude themselves into thinking that *violence* is sufficiently defined that we can pretend the use of violence has certain, inevitable psychological consequences.

Todd Allin Morman, writing in *Social Anarchism*, draws on Erich Fromm to make a tidy distinction between "rational authority" and "irrational authority." Morman asserts that "anarchism is against all forms of irrational authority and favors rational authority in its place."[16] Irrational authority is based on holding power over people, while rational authority is defined as influence voluntarily granted on the basis of experience and competence. "[I]t is impossible to employ violence to promote a higher anarchist order because violence necessarily reproduces psychological attitudes that are antithetical to the ends of anarchist revolution."

Quite typically, he argues that we should go into revolution peacefully, because if we do not, we will only "reconstitut[e] the state in a new...form." But why is it possible to stop being violent now, before the revolution, but not afterward? Why are we told that we would inevitably and powerlessly become authoritarian after a violent revolution, even as we are encouraged to break the psychological patterns of our violent society and forswear militant struggle? Morman does not answer how he can see humans deterministically at the end of a sentence, while treating humans as free agents in the beginning of the same sentence. I suspect it is because academics like Morman are afraid of what would happen to them if they did not give up militant revolution (which is to give up on revolution as a whole); instead, they prefer to assert their "rational authority" and pretend they are contributing to a process that will somehow make the state obsolete. Of course, our major theoretical contribution as anarchists is that the state was obsolete from its inception, but it holds and gains power nonetheless. Fromm's syllogism, or at least Morman's interpretation thereof, misses the point that to an "irrational authority," "rational authority" is irrelevant, meaningless, and powerless.

It seems to me that it would be much easier to end the psychological patterns of violence and domination once we had destroyed the social institutions, political bodies, and economic structures specifically constituted to perpetuate coercive domination. But proponents of nonviolence boldly sound the call to retreat, declaring that we should treat the symptoms while the disease is free to spread itself, defend itself, and vote itself pay raises. Morman says, "Violence is only capable of attacking the physical manifestations of the social relations that perpetuate the state. One cannot kill these social relations by a physical assault."[17] Leaving aside the fact that this point is blatantly false in relation to indigenous cultures' fighting off foreign invasion and imperialism (in which cases, killing or evicting the colonizer is indeed killing colonialism, if it can be done before Westernization has taken place), let us accept

Morman's narrow Eurocentrism and focus on societies in which oppressor and oppressed belong to the same nation or culture. He has just established that violence can destroy the physical but not the psychological manifestations of oppression. Any reasonable person would proceed by recommending a revolutionary struggle that contains both destructive and creative activities—violence against the oppressors and their machinery accompanied by simultaneous caretaking and healing of one's community. Morman and the thousands of pacifists who think like him instead declare that we should focus on psychological liberation while avoiding physical struggle. How they fail to see the concomitant parallel to the argument they have just made, that psychological actions cannot destroy the physical manifestations of the state, is baffling. Perhaps they believe that the social relationships of oppression are independent and create the physical structures of oppression out of whole cloth, but this is simplistic. The social relationships and physical structures cannot be fully separated (in reality, rather than in philosophy, for these terms are only analytical devices that make it easier to talk about different aspects of the same thing), and they clearly evolve in tandem. Physical structures and social relationships are mutually dependent, and mutually reinforcing.

Morman also holds on to a totalitarian idea of revolution. "The revolutionary is promoting one set of social relations and destroying old ones, not by teaching, example, or well-reasoned argument, but by power, fear, and intimidation: the buttresses of irrational authority."[18] This argument suggests that a nonpacifist revolution must be waged against people who are philosophically deviant or politically incorrect—people who *believe the wrong things* (this is how a political party views revolution). But there is more than one axis for liberation struggle. It can be cultural, to fight for the expulsion of a foreign colonizer and the bourgeois political parties that have taken on the characteristics of that colonizer (as described by Fanon), or it can be structural, to destroy centralized power structures and hierarchical institutions without targeting any actual people, other than those who choose to fight on the side of power. After a revolution that destroys all of the structures of capitalism—seizes all of the factories, redistributes all of the land, burns all of the money—people who are philosophically capitalist need not be purged or intimidated with irrational authority. Lacking a military apparatus to implement capitalism or a police apparatus to protect it, they—as people—are quite harmless, and will either learn to do something creative with their lives or starve to death without realizing that they can no longer pay someone to slave for them. Morman's typical pacifist-anarchist construction relies on a Eurocentric, political vision of revolution, in which a revolutionary party seizes power and enforces its vision of freedom on everyone else in the society through some centralized apparatus. In fact, it is society itself—as it stands now, an artificial binding together of people with no noncoerced common interests in working together—that needs to be destroyed. A militant revolutionary movement can destroy the central gravity of government that holds together mass polities in a single nation-state. After that point, we will not need some rational, "well-reasoned" ideology to hold everyone together, because societies will divide into smaller, organic units. Revolutionaries will not need to use violence to convince everyone to behave in a certain way because there will be no need for conformity across an entire country.

Morman's reasoning is also based on Western cultural assumptions that fail to appreciate any reason for violence not in the service of domination. These assumptions have much to do with the inherent totalitarianism of Western culture (which is also evident in the statist inclinations of pacifism, privileging state violence while actively ostracizing the violence of rebellion). The idea that the use of "violence" automatically constitutes an irrational authority does not make sense from the perspective of cultural values that do not necessarily portray violence as a tool in the service of domination. According to the Mande, Mangala the creator killed Farrow as a *sacrifice* in order to save what was left of creation. On the contrary, in Greek mythology, Cronus tried to kill his son, and later Zeus devoured his lover, Metis, to *maintain their power*. This dynamic is a pattern throughout Western mythologies. The use of violence is either calculated, to win power and coercive control, or impassioned, in which case the motivation is nearly always jealousy born out of the desire to possess another being. These patterns are not universal to all cultures.

They are also not universal to all situations. Collective, coordinated violence to establish and enforce a new set of social relations that must be preserved through violence, or revolution by way of taking over centralized institutions, does constitute the creation or preservation of a coercive authority. But these are not the only two options for social change. We have already seen Frantz Fanon describe violence as a "cleansing force" when used by people ground down and dehumanized by colonization to liberate themselves. (And the dynamics of colonialism apply today to indigenous populations, to outright colonies from Hawaii to Samoa, and to occupied areas from Kurdistan to Iraq, while similar dynamics apply to the populations of the neocolonies of Africa, Asia, and Latin America, and to the "internal colonies" descended from slave populations in the US. In short, these dynamics still apply to hundreds of millions of people and are not at all obsolete.) Fanon aided the FLN (National Liberation Front) in Algeria and worked in a psychiatric hospital, specializing in the psychology of the colonized and the psychological effects of their liberation struggles. In other words, he is somewhat better positioned than Erich Fromm to evaluate the psychology of violence in pursuit of liberation from the perspective of the majority of the world's population—not the vantage of an educated political party seeking to remake the world in its image, but the vantage of people subjugated to a system so violent that they can either forcefully fight back or displace that violence sociopathically against one another. Speaking of colonization and resistance to it, Fanon writes, "It is a commonplace that great social upheavals lessen the frequency of delinquency and mental disorders."[19]

To add to what is becoming a long list, nonviolence is deluded in repeating that means determine ends, as though never before has a transformation occurred in which end conditions were fundamentally different from the means that brought them about. After Red Cloud's War in 1866, for example, the Lakota did not descend into an orgy of violence because they had committed some moral/psychological transgression by killing white soldiers. On the contrary, they enjoyed nearly a decade of relative peace and autonomy until Custer invaded the Black Hills to find gold.[20] But instead of fitting the means (our tactics) to the situation we face, we are supposed to make our decisions based on conditions that are not even present, acting as though the revolution has already occurred and we live in that better world.[21] This wholesale renunciation of strategy forgets that neither of the lauded figureheads of nonviolence, Gandhi and King, believed that pacifism was a universally applicable panacea. Martin Luther King Jr. acknowledged that "[t]hose who make peaceful revolution impossible only make violent revolution inevitable."[22] Given the increased consolidation of the media (the presumed ally and moralizing tool of the nonviolent activist[23]) and the increased repressive powers of the government, can we really believe that a pacifist movement could overcome the government on a matter where compromise was unacceptable to ruling interests?

Closing out the list of common delusions is the all-too-frequent claim that violence alienates people. This is glaringly false. Violent video games and violent movies are the most popular. Even blatantly false wars win the support of at least half the population, often with the commentary that the US military is too humane and restrained to its enemies. On the other hand, self-righteous candlelight vigils are alienating to the majority of people who don't participate, who hurry by and smirk to themselves. Voting is alienating for the millions of people who know better than to participate and to some of the many people who participate for lack of better options. Showing a supposed "love" for "thy enemy" is alienating to people who know that love is something deeper, more intimate, than a superficial smiley face to be given out to six billion strangers simultaneously.[24] Pacifism is also alienating to the millions of lower-class Americans who silently cheer every time a cop or (especially) federal agent gets killed.[25] The real question is *who* is alienated by violence, and by what kind of violence? One anarchist writes:

> [E]ven if they *were*, who cares if the middle and upper classes are alienated by violence? They already had their violent revolution and we're living in it right now. Further, the whole notion that the middle and upper classes are alienated by violence is completely false...they support violence all the time, whether it is strikebreaking, police brutality, prisons, war, sanctions or capital punishment. What they really oppose is violence directed at dislodging them and their privileges."[26]

Reckless violence that subjects people to unnecessary risks without even striving to be effective or successful will most likely alienate people—especially those who already have to survive under the violence of oppression—but fighting for survival and freedom often wins sympathy. I have recently been fortunate enough to come into correspondence with Black Liberation Army prisoner Joseph Bowen, who got locked up after the cop who tried to kill him ended up dead. "Joe-Joe" won the respect of other prisoners after he and another prisoner assassinated the warden and deputy warden and wounded the guard commander at Philadelphia's Holmesburg Prison in 1973, in response to intense repression and religious persecution. In 1981, when a mass-escape attempt he helped organize at Graterford Prison was foiled and turned into a hostage situation, a huge amount of media attention was paid to the horrible conditions of Pennsylvania's prisons. During the five-day standoff, dozens of articles came out in the *Philadelphia Inquirer* and the national press, shedding light on the prisoners' grievances and underscoring the fact that these people who had nothing to lose would continue to fight against the repression and the bad conditions. Some corporate-media articles were even sym-pathetic toward Joe-Joe,[27] and in the end, the government agreed to transfer a dozen of the rebels to another prison, rather than storm in shooting—their preferred tactic. In fact, in the aftermath of the siege, Bowen had so upset the scales of political power that politicians were on the defensive and had to call for investiga-tions of conditions at Graterford Prison. In this and many other examples, including the Zapatistas in 1994 and the Appalachian miners in 1921, people humanize themselves precisely when they take up arms to fight against oppression.

Since the first edition of this book came out, I have been approached by many people who were not activists who told me how much they appreciated the sentiments herein. While activ-ists might assume these people are apathetic to the current social movements because they have never participated, I was told time and again that they wanted to get involved but didn't know how because the only organizing efforts they saw revolved around peaceful protests, which didn't feel inclusive to them and obvi-ously wouldn't accomplish anything. One working-class man told me how upon the US invasion of Iraq he jumped in his car and drove two hours to DC to take part in a protest, knowing no one else involved. When he arrived and saw a peaceful crowd herded by the police into a protest cage, he turned right around and drove home.

The frequent role of nonviolent activists in controlling or sabotaging revolutionary movements, and their failure to protect revolutionary activists from state repression, as well as their ap-peasement with the most hollow of "victories," suggests an ulte-rior motive to nonviolent activism. It seems to me that the most common motive is for pacifists to avail themselves of moral high ground and alleviate the substantial guilt they incur by recogniz-ing the many systems of oppression they are tied up in but fail to deal with in a meaningful way. Ward Churchill suggests that white pacifists wish to protect themselves from repression by consigning

their activism to posturing and formulating the social organization of a post-revolutionary world while people of color across the
world incur all the fatalities fighting for that world.[28] This is a far
cry from the solidarity role white pacifists imagine themselves to
be playing.

Nonviolent activism targeting the School of the Americas
(SOA) provides a good example. Organizing against the SOA
includes one of the largest sustained campaigns of civil disobedience in recent history, and it has drawn the participation and
support of a number of leading pacifists. During my involvement
with anti-SOA activism, I conceived of the civil disobedience and
prison sentence as a means of demonstrating the farcical and
authoritarian nature of the democratic process, and fostering
the escalation toward a truly revolutionary movement targeting
all aspects of capitalism and imperialism, not just the SOA. How
ridiculous would it be to campaign for the closure of a single
military school when numerous other institutions, indeed the
whole capitalist state structure, work toward the same ends? But
after the conclusion of my prison sentence, I saw that to the pacifist majority within the anti-SOA "movement," civil disobedience
was an end in itself, used for leverage in lobbying Congress and
recruiting new participants, and for alleviating privilege-induced
guilt and accessing the moral righteousness of those who have put
their money where their mouth is, so to speak. It enabled them
to claim that, by incurring a relatively easy prison sentence of six
months or less, they were "bearing witness" and "standing in solidarity with the oppressed" in Latin America.[29]

For all its fanfare, nonviolence is decrepit. Nonviolent theory
rests on a large number of manipulations, falsifications, and delusions. Nonviolent practice is ineffective and self-serving. In a
revolutionary sense, not only has nonviolence never worked, it
has never existed. Driving a car, eating meat, eating tofu, paying
rent, paying taxes, being nice to a cop—all of these are violent
activities.[30] The global system and everyone in it are soaked in

violence; it is enforced, coerced, involuntary. For those suffering under the violence of colonialism, military occupation, or racial oppression, nonviolence is not always an option—people must either fight back violently against their oppressor or displace that violence into anti-social violence against one another. Frantz Fanon writes:

> Here on the level of communal organizations we clearly discern the well-known behavior patterns of avoidance. It is as if plunging into a fraternal blood-bath allowed them to ignore the obstacle, and to put off till later the choice, nevertheless inevitable, which opens up the question of armed resistance to colonialism. Thus collective autodestruction in a very concrete form is one of the ways in which the native's muscular tension is set free.[31]

Peace is not an option until after the centrally organized violence that is the state is destroyed. Exclusive reliance on building alternatives—to sustain us, make the state obsolete, and heal us from this violence to prevent "autodestruction"—is also not an option, because the state can crush alternatives that cannot defend themselves. If we were allowed to live the change we wish to see in the world, there wouldn't be much need for revolution. Our options have been violently constrained to the following: actively supporting the violence of the system; tacitly supporting that violence by failing to challenge it; supporting some of the existing forceful attempts to destroy the system of violence; or pursuing new and original ways to *fight and destroy* that system. Privileged activists need to understand what the rest of the world's people have known all too long: we are in the midst of a war, and neutrality is not possible.[32] There is nothing in this world currently deserving of the name peace. Rather, it is a question of whose violence frightens us most, and on whose side we will stand.

7

THE ALTERNATIVE: POSSIBILITIES FOR REVOLUTIONARY ACTIVISM

I have made a number of forceful, even vitriolic, arguments against nonviolent activism, and I have not diluted these arguments. My goal has been to emphasize criticisms too often silenced, in order to defenestrate the stranglehold pacifism has over the movement's discourse—a stranglehold exerting such a monopoly over putative morality and strategic/tactical analysis in many circles as to preclude even the acknowledgment of a feasible alternative. Would-be revolutionaries need to realize that pacifism is so vapid and counterproductive that an alternative is imperative. Only then can we weigh the different paths of struggle fairly—and, I hope, in a more pluralistic, decentralized manner as well—rather than attempting to enforce a party line or the single correct revolutionary program.

My argument is not that all pacifists are apologists and sellouts without redeeming merit or a place in a revolutionary movement. Many pacifists are well-meaning would-be revolutionaries who have simply been unable to move past their cultural conditioning, which programs them instinctively to react to assaults on the Godlike state as the highest crime and treason. A handful of pacifists have shown such a sustained commitment to revolution and incurred such risks and sacrifices that they are above the criticisms typically deserved by pacifists, and even pose a challenge to the functioning of the status quo, particularly when their morals do not prevent them from working in solidarity with nonpacifist revolutionaries.[1] The point is that pacifism as ideology, with pretensions beyond a personal practice, incorrigibly serves state interests and is hopelessly wrapped up psychologically with the control schema of the patriarchy and white supremacy.

Now that I have demonstrated the need to replace a nonviolent revolutionary practice, I want to elaborate on what we might replace it with, as numerous nonpacifist forms of revolutionary struggle contain their own terminal flaws. In debate, pacifists typically generalize some broad faults of a few exemplified historical revolutions, avoid any detailed analysis, and rest their case. But rather than say, for instance, "See, the violent Russian Revolution led to another violent and authoritarian government, therefore violence is infectious,"[2] it would help to point out that all the Leninists wanted was an authoritarian, red-painted capitalist state with them at the head, and in their own terms they were quite successful.[3] We could also point out the contemporaneous anarchist revolutionaries in southern Ukraine, who consistently refused power and, for years, liberated huge areas from the Germans, the anti-Semitic nationalists, the Whites, and the Reds—but did not impose their will on those they liberated, whom they encouraged to self-organize.[4] Further leaving aside pacifism's mystifying, sweeping analysis, it might do well to dirty our hands in the historical details and analyze degrees of violence, perhaps by showing that in terms of structural depravity and state repression, Castro's Cuba, the product of a violent revolution, is arguably less violent than Batista's Cuba. However, there are already enough apologists for Castro as to disincline me from expending my energies in such a manner.

The common element of all of these authoritarian revolutions is their hierarchical form of organization. The authoritarianism of the USSR or People's Republic of China was not a mystical carryover from the violence they used, but a direct function of the hierarchies to which they were always wed. It is vague, meaningless, and ultimately untrue to say that violence always produces certain psychological patterns and social relationships. Hierarchy, however, is inseparable from psychological patterns and social relationships of domination. In fact, most of the violence in society that is unarguably wrong stems from coercive hierarchies. In other words, the concept of hierarchy has most of the analytical and moral precision that the concept of violence lacks. Therefore, to truly succeed, a liberation struggle must use any means necessary that are consistent with building a world free of coercive hierarchies.

This anti-authoritarianism must be reflected in both the organization and the ethos of a liberation movement. Organizationally, power must be decentralized—this means no political parties or bureaucratic institutions. Power should be located as much as possible in the grassroots—with individuals and in groups working within a community. Because grassroots and community groups are confined by real-life conditions and have constant contact with people outside the movement, ideology tends to flow upward, concentrating in "national committees" and other centralized levels of organization (which bring together like-minded people steeped in abstraction and removed from contact with most other folk's everyday realities). Few things have more potential for authoritarianism than a powerful ideology. Therefore, as much autonomy and decision-making power as possible must remain at the grassroots. When local groups do need to federate or otherwise coordinate over a wider geographic area—and the difficulty of this struggle will require coordination, discipline, pooling of resources, and common strategy—whatever organization arises should ensure that local groups do not lose their autonomy and that whatever higher levels of organization are created (such as the regional or national committees of a federation) are weak, temporary, frequently replaced, recallable, and always dependent on ratification by the local groups. Otherwise, those who fill the higher levels of organization are likely to develop a bureaucratic mindset, and the organization is likely to develop interests of its own, which will soon diverge from the interests of the movement.

Additionally, no organization should monopolize the movement. Organizations should not be empires; they should be temporary tools that overlap, proliferate, and die out when they are no longer needed. A movement will be healthier and harder to co-opt if there is a diversity of groups filling different niches and pursuing similar purposes;[5] and these groups will be less prone to infighting if people within the movement tend to belong to multiple groups rather than giving their loyalty to a single group.

The culture, or ethos, of the liberation movement is also vital. Noncoercive structures are easily subverted if the culture and desires of the people operating those structures draw them toward other ends. For starters, a culture of liberation must favor pluralism over monopoly. In terms of struggle, this means we must abandon the idea that there is only one right way, that we must get everyone to sign on to the same platform or join the same organization. On the contrary, the struggle will benefit from a plurality of strategies attacking the state from different angles. This does not mean that everyone should work alone or at cross-purposes. We need to coordinate and unify as much as possible to increase our collective strength, but we should also reconsider how much uniformity is actually possible. It is impossible to get everyone to agree that one strategy for struggle is the best, and indeed this contention is probably wrong. After all, different people have different strengths and experiences and face different aspects of oppression: it only makes sense that there should be different paths of struggle on which we fight simultaneously toward liberation. The authoritarian monotheism inherent in Western civilization would lead us to view these other paths as unintelligent detours, as competition—we might even try to repress these other tendencies within the movement. Anti-authoritarianism requires that we abandon this mindset, recognize the inevitability of differences, and think of people who deviate from us as allies. After all, we are not trying to impose one new, utopian society on everybody after the revolution; the goal is to destroy centralized power structures so each community has the autonomy to organize itself in the way that all its members collectively decide will best enable them to meet their needs, while also joining or leaving free associations of mutual aid with communities around them.[6] Everyone has an innate potential for freedom and self-organization; therefore, if we identify as anarchists, our job is not to convert everyone else to anarchism, but to use our perspectives and collective experiences to guard against the co-optation efforts of the institutional Left and to provide models for autonomous social relationships and self-organization in cultures where none currently exist.

There is also the question of leadership in an anti-authoritarian struggle. The traditional idea of leadership, as an institutionalized or coercive role, as holding power over people, is hierarchical and inhibitive of people's growth. But it is also true that people are not equal in terms of abilities, that this revolution will take a tremendous amount of expertise, and that smart, nonegotistical people will voluntarily place someone with more expertise than others in a position of noncoercive and temporary leadership. The approach of an anti-authoritarian ethos toward leadership is that power needs to be constantly redistributed outwards. It is the responsibility of people who find themselves in positions of leadership to lend their talents to the movement while spreading their leadership around, teaching other people rather than holding on to their expertise as a form of power.

Additionally, an anti-authoritarian ethos favors fighting uncompromisingly against oppression, but opposes crushing those who have been defeated; it favors reconciliation over punishment.

With these structures and culture, a liberation movement has a better chance of succeeding without creating a new authoritarian system. There will always be a tension between being effective and being liberating, and in the complexity of struggle there is plenty of grey space, but it helps to see cultivating an anti-authoritarian practice as a constant battle between two requirements (efficiency and freedom) that are conflicting but not mutually exclusive. The pacifist vision of struggle, based on a polar dichotomy between violence and nonviolence, is unrealistic and self-defeating.

More concretely, it is hard to generalize how a liberation movement using a diversity of tactics should conduct its struggle. Specific groups need to decide that for themselves based on the conditions they face—not based on the prescriptions of some ideology. In all likelihood, though, an anti-authoritarian liberation movement would need to emphasize building an autonomous culture that can resist the mind control of the corporate media and a foundation of social centers, free schools, free clinics, community agriculture, and other structures that can support communities in resistance. Westernized people also need to develop collective social relationships. For those growing up in the Global North, being an anarchist provides no exception to being imbued with individualistic, punishment- and privilege-based forms of social interactions. We need to employ working models of restorative or transformative justice so that we truly don't need police or prisons. As long as we are dependent on the state, we will never overthrow it.

Readers may notice that some of the major initial requirements of a liberation movement do not include "violent" actions. I hope that by now we can abandon the dichotomy between violence and nonviolence altogether. The use of violence is not a stage in the struggle that we must work toward and pass through in order to win. It does not help to isolate violence. Rather, we must be aware of certain types of repression we will probably have to face, certain tactics we will probably have to use. At every stage in the struggle we must cultivate a militant spirit. Our social centers should honor militant activists in prison, or those killed by the state; our free schools should teach self-defense and the history of struggle. If we wait to bring in militancy until the state has increased repression to the level that it is blatantly obvious that they have declared war on us, it will be too late. Cultivating militancy should go hand in hand with preparation and outreach.

It is dangerous to become totally cut off from a mainstream reality by rushing into tactics that no one else can understand, much less support. People who act prematurely and cut themselves off from popular support will be easy for the government to pick off.[7] That said, we cannot let our actions be determined by what is acceptable in the mainstream. The opinions of the mainstream are conditioned by the state; pandering to the mainstream is pandering to the state. Rather, we must work to escalate militancy, to educate through exemplary actions, and to increase the level of militancy acceptable (to at least segments of the population we have identified as potential supporters). Radicals from a privileged background have the most work to do in this regard because these communities have the most conservative reactions to militant tactics. Privileged radicals seem to be more likely to ask, "What would society think?" as an excuse for their passivity.

Increasing the acceptance of militant tactics is not easy work, we must gradually bring people to accept more militant forms of struggle. If the only choice we can give is between bomb throwing and voting, almost all of our potential allies will choose voting. And though more cultural conditioning must be overcome before people can accept and practice more dangerous, deadly tactics, such tactics cannot be placed at the top of some hierarchy. Fetishizing violence neither improves a movement's effectiveness nor preserves its anti-authoritarian qualities.

Because of the nature of the state, any struggle for liberation will probably eventually become an armed struggle. In fact, a good many peoples are engaged in armed struggle to liberate themselves right now, including the Iraqis, the Palestinians, the Ijaw in Nigeria, some indigenous nations in South America and Papua New Guinea, and, to a lesser extent, anti-authoritarian groups in Greece, Italy, and elsewhere. As I write this sentence, indigenous activists, anarchists, and unionists armed with just bricks and clubs are holding the barricades in Oaxaca against an impending military assault. Several of them have already been killed, and, as the military strikes again and again, they must decide whether to escalate tactics to improve their capability for self-defense, at the risk of graver consequences. I won't say that armed struggle is an ideological necessity, but for many people in many places it does become a necessity to overthrow, or simply defend against, the state. It would be wonderful if most people did not have to go through a process of armed struggle to liberate themselves, and, given the extent to which economies and governments are integrated globally these days, a good many governments might easily collapse if they were already weakened by spreading waves of global revolt. But some people will have to experience armed struggle, some have to even now, and it would be unforgivable if our strategy for revolution banked on the certainty that other people will die in bloody conflicts while we remain safe.

We must realistically accept that revolution is a social war, not because we like war, but because we recognize that the status quo is a low-intensity war and challenging the state results in an intensification of that warfare. We must also accept that revolution necessitates interpersonal conflict because certain classes of people are employed to defend the centralizing institutions we must destroy. People who continue to dehumanize themselves as agents of law and order must be defeated by whatever means necessary until they can no longer prevent people's autonomous realization of their needs. I hope that during this process we can build a culture of respect for our enemies (a number of non-Western cultures have shown it is indeed possible to respect a person or animal you must kill), which will help to prevent purges or a new authority when the present state has been defeated. For example, it could be seen as acceptable to kill a more powerful enemy (for instance, someone who must be targeted clandestinely for fear of state reprisal), unfavorable to kill someone who is equally powerful (such that it would only be seen as justified by one's peers in pitched circumstances and self-defense), and downright immoral and scornful to kill someone weaker (for instance, someone already defeated).

We can succeed at feasible revolutionary activism by striving toward undiluted, long-term goals, but we must not forget short-term victories. In the meantime, people need to survive and be nourished. And we must recognize that violent struggle against an extremely powerful enemy in which long-term victory may seem impossible can lead to small short-term victories. Losing fights can be better than not fighting at all; fighting empowers people and teaches us that we *can* fight. Referring to the defeat at the Battle of Blair Mountain during the 1921 Mine War in West Virginia, filmmaker John Sayles writes, "the psychological victory of those violent days may have been more important. When a colonized people learn they can fight back together, life can never again be so comfortable for their exploiters."[8]

With enough bold, empowering resistance, we can move beyond small victories to achieve a lasting victory against the state, the patriarchy, capitalism, and white supremacy. Revolution is imperative, and revolution necessitates struggle. There are many effective forms of struggle, and some of these methods can lead to the worlds we dream of. To find one of the right paths, we must observe, assess, criticize, communicate, and, above all, learn by doing.

INTRODUCTION

1. Some periodicals limited to the strictly anarchist milieu, such as *Anarchy: A Journal of Desire Armed*, are not at all pacifist. However, their influence, and the influence of their readership, can be clearly seen as marginal in areas where, otherwise, anarchists have a major impact. At mass mobilizations of the anti-war and anti-globalization movements, in which anarchists are key organizers, criticisms of pacifism are not even entertained; at best, some participants can successfully argue that watered-down forms of direct action really do qualify as nonviolent. Media widely available beyond anarchist circles, in the way progressive media are somewhat available to the mainstream, are almost exclusively pacifist, even when many of the volunteers that keep those media alive are anti-authoritarians who support a diversity of tactics.

E N D N O T E S

2. Because it may be presumptuous to refer to someone who is not engaged in open conflict with the state as a revolutionary, I define a *revolutionary activist* as someone who, at the least, is building toward the point when such a conflict is practical. Some people have qualms with the term *activist*, or associate it with reformist types of activism. To avoid being too particular about words and terminology, I will ask readers simply to receive this term in the best possible way.

CHAPTER ONE—NONVIOLENCE IS INEFFECTIVE

1. This particular list comes from an article written by Spruce Houser (Spruce Houser, "Domestic Anarchist Movement Increasingly Espouses Violence," *Athens News*, August 12, 2004, http://athensnews.com/index. php?action=viewarticle&section=archive&story_id=17497), a peace activist and self-proclaimed anarchist. I have seen these same putative victories declared by other pacifists time and again.

2. Hello NYC, *2/15: The Day the World Said No to War* (Oakland, CA: AK Press, 2003). This book gives one a feel for the way peace activists celebrate these protests.

3. For example, as soon as a pacifist panelist at the anarchist conference mentioned in the introduction was forced to admit that the civil rights

struggle did not end victoriously, he changed directions without blinking an eye and blamed the struggle's failure on militant liberation movements, saying that as the movement *became* violent, it started to lose ground. This argument ignores the fact that resistance against slavery and racial oppression was militant well before the late 1960s, and also disavows any specific analysis that might, say, correspond an increasing militancy with a decreasing base. Such correlations are factually nonexistent.

4. Chandrasekhar Azad, who was killed in a shootout with the British, is a focal point of a recent movie, *The Last Revolutionary*, by Indian director Priyadarshan.

5. Reeta Sharma, "What if Bhagat Singh Had Lived?" *The Tribune of India*, March 21, 2001; http://www.tribuneindia.com/2001/20010321/edit.htm#6. It is important to note that people across India beseeched Gandhi to ask for the commutation of Bhagat Singh's death sentence, given for the assassination of a British official, but Gandhi strategically chose not to speak out against the state execution, which many believe he easily could have stopped. Thus was a rival revolutionary removed from the political landscape.

6. Bose resigned after a conflict with other Indian political leaders, stemming from Gandhi's opposition to Bose because the latter did not support nonviolence. For more on Indian liberation struggles, read Sumit Sarkar, *Modern India: 1885–1947* (New York: St. Martin's Press, 1989).

7. Professor Gopal K, e-mail to author, September 2004. Gopal also writes, "I have friends in India who still haven't forgiven Gandhi for this."

8. Though the conservatism inherent in any political establishment prevented many Euro/American states from seeing this for some time, neocolonial rule is much more efficient at enriching the colonizer than direct colonial administration, and more efficient at maintaining power, once direct colonialism has successfully effected the necessary political and economic reorganization within the colonies. Liberals within the imperialist states, unfairly characterized as disloyal or unpatriotic, were, in fact, right on the money when they advocated independence for the colonies. George Orwell, Ho Chi Minh, and others have written about the fiscal inefficiency of colonialism. See Ho Chi Minh, "The Failure of French Colonization," in *Ho Chi Minh on Revolution*, ed. Bernard Fall (New York: Signet Books, 1967).

9. India's neocolonial status is widely documented as part of the expanding body of anti- and alter-globalist literature. See Arundhati Roy, *Power Politics* (Cambridge: South End Press, 2002) and Vandana Shiva, *Stolen Harvest* (Cambridge: South End Press, 2000).

10. The group Direct Action in Canada and the Swiss guerrilla Marco Camenisch are two examples.

11. See Robert Williams, *Negroes with Guns* (Chicago: Third World Press, 1962); Kathleen Cleaver and George Katsiaficas, *Liberation, Imagination, and the Black Panther Party* (New York: Routledge, 2001); and Charles Hamilton and Kwame Ture, *Black Power: The Politics of Liberation in America* (New York: Random House, 1967).

12. "Historical Context of the Founding of the Party," http://www.blackpanther.org/legacynew.htm. In 1994, Dr. Kenneth Clark, the psychologist whose testimony was instrumental in winning the 1954 *Brown v. Board of Education* Supreme Court decision, stated that segregation was worse than it had been 40 years prior. Also see Suzzane Goldberg, "US wealth gap grows for ethnic minorities," *The Guardian (UK)* October 19, 2004, reprinted in *Asheville Global Report*, no. 302 (2004) http://www.agrnews.org/issues/302/nationalnews.html. The Pew Hispanic Center, analyzing US Census data, recently found that the average white family has a net worth 11 times greater than that of the average Latino family, and 14 times greater than that of the average black family, and that the disparity is growing.

13. Mick Dumke, "Running on Race," *ColorLines*, Fall 2004, 17–19. This article was written before Barack Obama's election so I have updated the figure.

14. "They [the civil rights movement and the black liberation/anti-colonial movement] rapidly evolved toward armed struggle, with self-defense leading to armed organizations. Anti-government violence had mass approval and participation." E. Tani and Kaé Sera, *False Nationalism, False Internationalism* (Chicago: A Seeds Beneath the Snow Publication, 1985), 94. Also see Mumia Abu-Jamal, *We Want Freedom* (Cambridge: South End Press, 2004), 32, 65.

15. Flores Alexander Forbes, "Point Number 7: We Want an Immediate End to Police Brutality and the Murder of Black People; Why I Joined the Black Panther Party," in *Police Brutality: An Anthology*, ed. Jill Nelson (New York: W.W. Norton and Company, 2000), 237.

16. Abu-Jamal, *We Want Freedom*, 31.

17. "[I]f an oppressed people's pent-up emotions are not nonviolently released, they will be violently released. So let the Negro march....For if his frustrations and despair are allowed to continue piling up, millions of Negroes will seek solace and security in Black nationalist ideologies." Martin Luther King Jr., quoted in Tani and Sera, *False Nationalism*, 107.

Martin Luther King Jr. played up the threat of black revolutionary violence as the likely outcome if the state did not meet his reformist demands, and his organizers often capitalized on riots carried out by militant black activists to put the pacifist black leaders in a more favorable light. See especially Ward Churchill, *Pacifism as Pathology* (Winnipeg: Arbeiter Ring, 1998), 43.

18. Tani and Sera, *False Nationalism*, 96–104. As King himself said, "The sound of the explosion in Birmingham reached all the way to Washington."

19. Ward Churchill, *Pacifism as Pathology*. Also, for an example, Tani and Sera, *False Nationalism*, chapter 6.

20. A pacifist panelist at the North American Anarchist Conference, rejecting the idea that the Vietnamese resistance, and not the peace movement, defeated the US, temporarily confused his moral/tactical position with a racial one by pointing out that it was US troops assassinating their officers that also led to the end of the war.

21. Tani and Sera, *False Nationalism*, 124–125. "Project 100,000" was begun in 1966 at the suggestion of White House adviser Daniel Patrick Moynihan, who, incidentally, hypothesized that the unemployed men targeted for military service were "maladapted" because of "disorganized and matrifocal family life," while Vietnam represented "a world away from women." (Interestingly, demonization of strong black women was eventually insinuated into the Black Power movement itself). Colonel William Cole, commander of an Army recruiting district, said, "President Johnson wanted those guys off the street."

22. Tani and Sera, *False Nationalism*, 127.

23. Matthew Rinaldi, *Olive-Drab Rebels: Subversion of the US Armed Forces in the Vietnam War*, rev. ed. (London: Antagonism Press, 2003), 17.

24. Ibid., 11–13.

25. Tani and Sera, *False Nationalism*, 117–118.

26. It is educational to see how the elite themselves perceived the anti-war movement. One rich account comes from Secretary of Defense Robert McNamara in the documentary *Fog of War: Eleven Lessons from the Life of Robert S. McNamara*, directed by Errol Morris, 2003. McNamara clearly expressed being troubled by the protests often held outside his workplace, but with the typical arrogance of a bureaucrat assumed the public didn't know enough to make policy suggestions. He believed that he too wanted peace, and as a leading government expert he was thus working in the interests of the anti-war protestors.

27. "Millions Give Dramatic Rebuff to US War Plans," News, United for Peace and Justice, http://www.unitedforpeace.org/article.php?id=1070 (accessed October 5, 2006). Originally published by Agence France-Presse, February 16, 2003.

28. Excluding Al Sharpton, who was treated (as always) as a pariah.

29. Sinikka Tarvainen, "Spain's Aznar Risks All for a War in Iraq," Deutsche Presse-Agentur, March 11, 2003.

30. Not only were commentators nearly unanimous in attributing the shift of power directly to the bombings, the Spanish government itself acknowledged the impact of the bombings by trying to cover up Al-Qaida involvement, instead blaming ETA Basque separatists. Members of the government knew that if the bombings were connected in the public mind to Spanish participation in the Iraq occupation, they would lose in the polls, as they did.

31. Ward Churchill, in using the example of the Holocaust to demonstrate the pathology of pacifism in the face of oppression, cites Raul Hilberg, *The Destruction of the European Jews*, (Chicago: Quadrangle, 1961) and Isaiah Trunk, *Judenrat: The Jewish Councils in Eastern Europe Under Nazi Occupation* (New York: Macmillan, 1972). Churchill's own contributions to the topic, which informed my own, can be found in Churchill, *Pacifism as Pathology*, 31–37. He also recommends Bruno Bettleheim's Foreword to Miklos Nyiszli, *Auschwitz* (New York: Fawcett Books, 1960).

32. The example of the Danes during the Holocaust was used by pacifist anarchist Colman McCarthy at his workshop "Pacifism and Anarchism" at the National Conference on Organized Resistance, American University (Washington, DC), February 4, 2006.

33. Yehuda Bauer, *They Chose Life: Jewish Resistance in the Holocaust* (New York: The American Jewish Committee, 1973) 32, 33.

34. Ibid., 21.

35. Ibid., 36.

36. For example, on a listserv of former "prisoners of conscience" with School of the Americas Watch (SOAW), a group that has conducted one of the longest-running campaigns of nonviolent civil disobedience against US foreign policy, one veteran pacifist suggested that if the military was placing more restrictions on protesting outside an Army base that had been targeted by demonstrations, we were doing something wrong, and should take a step back. The same person, representative of a large trend within US pacifism, also objected to calling a protest a "march" instead of a walk (although he claimed to uphold the legacy of King and Gandhi).

37. Bauer, *They Chose Life*, 45.

38. Ibid., 39–40.

39. Ibid., 39 (regarding Kovno), 41 (regarding France).

40. Ibid., 47–48.

41. Ibid., 50.

42. Ibid., 52–53.

43. Ibid., 53–54.

44. One example of the mere threat of popular violence creating change comes from the American Indian Movement (AIM), in Gordon, Nebraska in 1972. An Oglala man, Raymond Yellow Thunder, had been killed by white people whom police refused to arrest (this was a relatively common occurrence). His relatives, fed up with the apathy of the government, called in AIM. Thirteen hundred angry Indians occupied the town of Gordon for three days, threatening: "We've come here to Gordon today to secure justice for American Indians and to put Gordon on the map…and if justice is not immediately forthcoming, we'll be back to take Gordon off the map." [Ward Churchill and Jim Vander Wall, *Agents of Repression: The FBI's Secret Wars Against the Black Panther Party and the American Indian Movement* (Cambridge: South End Press, 1990), 122.] Promptly, the two murderers were arrested, a cop was suspended, and local authorities made some effort to end discrimination against Indians.

CHAPTER TWO—NONVIOLENCE IS RACIST

1. See, for example, Malcolm, X, "Twenty Million Black People in a Political, Economic, and Mental Prison," in *Malcolm X: The Last Speeches*, ed. Bruce Perry (New York: Pathfinder, 1989), 23–54.

2. In one conversation I had with a pacifist Mandela was held up as an exemplary person of color and abandoned just as quickly when I mentioned Mandela's embrace of armed struggle. [Detailed in his autobiography: Nelson Mandela, *Long Walk to Freedom: The Autobiography of Nelson Mandela* (Boston: Little, Brown, 1995)].

3. Jack Gilroy, e-mail, January 23, 2006. This particular e-mail was the culmination of a rather sordid conversation on the listserv of a white pacifist group, during which participants discussed a suggested civil rights–style march through the heart of the black South. One person suggested calling it a "walk" instead of a "march," because "march" constitutes "violent language." Gilroy asserted, "Of course we are claiming the mantle of Dr. King!" This latter was in response to a criticism made by a black activist, who said that by holding such a march (it was supposed to start in Birmingham or another city of equal

symbolism), they were co-opting King's legacy and would probably offend and alienate black people (given that the organization was predominantly white, downplayed race in its analysis, and focused on oppression occurring abroad while missing, for instance, the fact that the civil rights movement is still continuing at home). The white peace veteran responded in an extremely condescending and insulting way to the criticism, even calling the black activist "boy" and claiming that the pacifist movement was so white because people of color "have not listened, have not taught when they have learned, have not preached from their pulpit...have not been able to connect to our movement to bring justice to all people of Latin America—which includes millions of people of color." He finished off the same e-mail by insisting that the fight against injustice "has no color bar."

4. Rev. Dr. Martin Luther King Jr., interview by Alex Haley, *Playboy*, January 1965. http://www.playboy.com/arts-entertainment/features/mlk/index.html.

5. Malcolm X, quoted in Abu-Jamal, *We Want Freedom*, 41. For more of Malcolm X's then-crucial analysis, see George Breitman, ed., *Malcolm X Speaks* (New York: Grove Press, 1965).

6. Tani and Sera, *False Nationalism*, 106.

7. Abu-Jamal, *We Want Freedom*, 262.

8. Allegations of government involvement in Malcolm X's assassination are convincingly presented by George Breitman, Herman Porter, and Baxter Smith in *The Assassination of Malcolm X* (New York: Pathfinder Press, 1976).

9. Ward Churchill and Jim Vander Wall, *The COINTELPRO Papers: Documents from the FBI's Secret Wars Against Dissent in the United States* (Cambridge: South End Press, 1990).

10. I know that personally, despite being interested in history and taking advanced placement US history classes throughout my years in some of the better public schools in the nation, I graduated high school knowing little about Malcolm X, other than that he was an "extremist" black Muslim. However, as early as elementary school, I knew quite a bit about Martin Luther King Jr. To be fair, Malcolm X is as important, if not more important, a figure to the civil rights and black liberation movements as King. In subsequent years, my political education in progressive white circles failed to correct either the white-out of Malcolm X or the misleading hagiography of King. It was only upon reading in black activists' writings of the importance of Malcolm X that I did the necessary research.

11. Darren Parker, e-mail, July 10, 2004.

12. Consider the popularity, for instance, of the following quote: "What these white people do not realize is that Negroes who riot have given up on America. When nothing is done to alleviate their plight, this merely confirms the Negroes' conviction that America is a hopelessly decadent society." Martin Luther King Jr., "A Testament of Hope" in James Melvin Washington, ed., A Testament of Hope: The Essential Writings of Martin Luther King, Jr. (San Francisco: Harper & Row, 1986), 324.

13. This sentiment, though it has been expressed by many different people, comes to me most directly from Roger White, *Post Colonial Anarchism* (Oakland: Jailbreak Press, 2004). White primarily addresses white anarchists' frequent tendency to shun national liberation movements for not conforming to a particular anarchist ideology. The dynamic is similar to the one created by pacifism, which I describe, and both are more functions of whiteness than any particular ideology. Pacifism has been one stumbling block that has allowed white radicals to control or sabotage liberation movements, but it is by no means the only one. White's book is worth a read, precisely because militant white anarchists encounter many of the same problems as white pacifists.

14. Tani and Sera, *False Nationalism*, 134–137.

15. Ibid., 137–161.

16. Abu-Jamal, *We Want Freedom*, 7.

17. Personal e-mail to author, December 2003.

18. David Cortright, "The Power of Nonviolence," *The Nation*, February 18, 2002, http://www.thenation.com/doc/20020218/cortright. This article attributes a one-word quote to César Chávez, but it is left to white pacifists to explain the meaning and implementation of nonviolent strategies.

19. Bob Irwin and Gordon Faison, "Why Nonviolence? Introduction to Theory and Strategy," Vernal Project, 1978, http://www.vernalproject.org/OPapers/WhyNV/WhyNonviolence1.html.

20. Staughton Lynd and Alice Lynd, *Nonviolence in America: A Documentary History* (Maryknoll, New York: Orbis Books, 1995).

21. Quotes from white organizers at the time, in Ward Churchill, *Pacifism as Pathology*. 60–62.

22. Art Gish, "Violence/Nonviolence" (panel discussion, North American Anarchist Conference, Athens, OH, August 13, 2004).

23. Tani and Sera, *False Nationalism,* 101–102.

24. Belinda Robnett, *How Long? How Long? African-American Women in the Struggle for Civil Rights* (Oxford: Oxford University Press, 1997), 184–186.

25. Kristian Williams, *Our Enemies in Blue* (Brooklyn: Soft Skull Press, 2004), 87.

26. Ibid., 266.

27. Keith McHenry, e-mail, international Food Not Bombs listserv, April 20, 2006.

28. Frantz Fanon, *The Wretched of the Earth* (New York: Grove Press, 1963), 86.

29. Ibid., 94.

30. Darren Parker, e-mail, July 10, 2004.

31. Churchill and Vander Wall, *Agents of Repression*, 188.

32. Some of the most dedicated nonviolent activists in the US have faced torture and murder in the course of Latin American solidarity work. But this is not quite the same thing as what activists of color face within the US, given that these white activists have faced violence in a situation they sought out rather than one imposed on them, their families, and their communities. It is, after all, much easier to have a martyr complex for oneself than for one's family (which is not to say that all of these activists were motivated by such a complex, though I have certainly met a few who cash in that risk to claim that they have experienced oppression rivaling that felt by people of color).

33. Churchill, *Pacifism as Pathology*, 60–61.

34. David Gilbert, *No Surrender: Writings from an Anti-Imperialist Political Prisoner* (Montreal: Abraham Guillen Press, 2004), 22–23.

35. Alice Woldt, quoted in Chris McGann, "Peace Movement Could Find Itself Fighting Over Tactics," *Seattle Post-Intelligencer*, February 21, 2003, http://seattlepi.nwsource.com/local/109590_peacemovement21.shtml.

36. E-mail to author, October 2004. This same activist paternalistically rewrote the history of black liberation to declare that the Black Panthers did not advocate violence. In the same e-mail, he quoted from Sun Tzu's *Art of War* to bolster his case and improve his tactical sophistication. Whether Sun Tzu would have agreed with his theories' being used in an argument for the efficacy of pacifism is questionable.

37. E-mail to author, October 2004.

38. David Dellinger, "The Black Rebellions," in *Revolutionary Nonviolence: Essays by David Dellinger* (New York: Anchor, 1971), 207. In the same essay, Dellinger admits that "there are occasions when those who act nonviolently themselves must become reluctant allies or critical supporters of those who resort to violence."

39. Gilbert, *No Surrender*, 23.

40. Abu-Jamal, *We Want Freedom*, 76.

41. Belinda Robnett points out that by becoming more militant and adopting a Black Power ideology, previously nonviolent groups such as SNCC "led liberal financial supporters [presumably mostly white] to stop contributing." This loss of mainstream funding led in part to the collapse of the organization (Robnett, *How Long?* 184–186). Robnett, however, equates the abandonment of nonviolence with machismo. Reflecting her academic status (as a sociology professor in the University of California system), she blurs the line between FBI-paid provocateurs advocating sexism within the movement (for example, Ron Karenga) and legitimate activists advocating increased militancy, or legitimate activists who did, in fact, confuse militancy with machismo. She also mentions that Angela Davis complained about being criticized by militant black nationalists "for doing a 'man's job'" (Robnett, *How Long?* 183), but she neglects to mention that Davis was highly influential in advocating militant struggle. Robnett also seems to neglect mentioning how problematic it is when groups with such radical agendas as racial equality are not self-sustaining and instead rely on the support of the federal government and white donors.

CHAPTER THREE—NONVIOLENCE IS STATIST

1. On February 9, 2006, a member of the nonviolent group SOA Watch (which attracts support from a range of groups, from progressives to anarchists) suggested on an e-mail list that because police had been dealing with the annual demonstration outside Fort Benning in Georgia more aggressively in recent years, the group should move the demonstration into some public place away from the military base to avoid confrontation. He wrote, "Wherever polarization takes place, it's time, in my opinion, for the peace campaign to re-evaluate its tactics. Relationships are at the core of peacemaking. 'We' and 'Them' can lead ultimately to war. 'Us' has a better chance for achieving negotiable (nonviolent) solutions and can lead ultimately to a culture of peace."

2. In one recent example, flyers being passed out by the thousands at the protests against the 2004 Republican National Convention claimed that anyone advocating violence was likely a police agent.

3. Churchill and Vander Wall, *Agents of Repression*, 94–99, 64–77. In the case of Jonathan Jackson, it seems that the FBI and police instigated the entire plot in an attempt to assassinate the most militant California Panthers. They encouraged a hostage-taking at the Marin County courthouse, but only because they were prepared with a large team of sharpshooters ready

to neutralize the militants. Yet "not taking the bait" (this phrase is used as though all advocates of militancy are provocateurs—a dangerous, and potentially violent, charge that has been leveled against many) will not keep anyone safe. FBI informer William O'Neal encouraged the Illinois Panthers, whom he had infiltrated, to take part in such bizarre plots as obtaining nerve gas or an airplane to bomb city hall. When they would not, the FBI went ahead and assassinated Panther leader Fred Hampton anyway.

4. Two good books about the COINTELPRO repression are Churchill and Vander Wall's *Agents of Repression* and Abu-Jamal's *We Want Freedom*. On similar repression abroad, read William Blum, *Killing Hope: US Military and CIA Interventions since World War II* (Monroe, Maine: Common Courage Press, 1995).

5. The repression of the ELF, termed the "Green Scare," and the imprisonment of the Stop Huntingdon Animal Cruelty (SHAC) activists were widely reported in radical and environmental media. See, for example, Brian Evans, "Two ELF Members Plead Guilty to 2001 Arson," *Asheville Global Report*, no. 404 (October 12, 2006): http://www.agrnews. org/?section=archives&cat_id=48&article_id=1296; and "The SHAC 7," http://www.shac7.com/case.htm.

6. A May 3, 2006, search of the archives of two leftist, nonmilitant independent-media websites, Common Dreams and AlterNet, revealed the predicted disparity. I searched for two phrases, the "Thomas Merton Center" and "Filiberto Ojeda Ríos." The first search for the Thomas Merton Center for Peace and Justice, one of the targets of a relatively nonintrusive campaign through which the FBI surveilled peace groups, as revealed by ACLU investigations early in 2006, brought up 23 articles on Common Dreams and five on AlterNet. The search on Filiberto Ojeda Ríos, a former leader of the Macheteros, a group within the Puerto Rican independence movement, who was assassinated by the FBI on September 23, 2005, brought up one article on Common Dreams and zero on AlterNet. Although few people on the mainland showed any concern, tens of thousands of Puerto Ricans marched in San Juan to protest the killing. Those two websites contained considerably fewer articles on the waves of violent FBI raids against Puerto Rican independence activists occurring in February 2006 than on the revelation, publicized at about the same time, that the FBI in Texas was spying on the predominantly white group Food Not Bombs as part of its counterterrorism activities. For coverage of the spying on the white peace activists, see "Punished for Pacifism," *Democracy Now*, Pacifica Radio, March 15, 2006. For coverage of the FBI assassination

and subsequent raids in Puerto Rico, see the "September 30th Newsbriefs" (2005) and "February 28th Newsbriefs" (2006) on SignalFire, www.signalfire. org. Both events were covered by Indymedia Puerto Rico (for example, CMI-PR, "Fuerza Bruta Imperialista Allana Hogar de Compañera, Militantes Boricuas le Dan lo Suyo," Indymedia Puerto Rico, February 10, 2006, http://pr.indymedia.org/news/2006/02/13197.php).

7. Abu-Jamal, *We Want Freedom*, 262–263.

8. Churchill and Vander Wall, *Agents of Repression*, 364.

9. Federal Bureau of Investigation, *FBI Intelligence Bulletin No. 89* (October 15, 2003). Available online at http://www.signalfire.org/resources/FBImemo.pdf.

10. Ibid.

11. Greg White, "US Military Planting Stories in Iraqi Newspapers," *Asheville Global Report*, no. 360 (December 7, 2005): http://www.agrnews. org/?section=archives&cat_id=10&article_id=194.

12. Fanon, *The Wretched of the Earth*, 61–62.

13. William Cran, "88 Seconds in Greensboro," *Frontline*, PBS, January 24, 1983.

14. "American Legion Declares War on Peace Movement," *Democracy Now*, Pacifica Radio, August 25, 2005. At the American Legion's national convention in 2005, the 3-million-strong organization voted to use whatever means necessary to end "public protest" and ensure "the united backing" of the US population for the War on Terror.

15. During and after World War I, the American Legion was an important paramilitary force in helping the government repress anti-war activists and labor organizers, particularly the Wobblies (IWW, Industrial Workers of the World). In 1919, in Centralia, Washington, they castrated and lynched Wesley Everest of the IWW.

16. Glenn Thrush, "Protest a 'Privilege,' Mayor Bloomberg Says," *NY Newsday*, August 17, 2004, http://www.unitedforpeace.org/article. php?id=2557. Commenting on the protests against the 2004 Republican National Convention in NYC, Mayor Bloomberg called free speech a privilege that can be taken away if abused. There are numerous other incidents of officials being so candid, and a whole history of episodes involving the government's denial of free speech and other civil and human rights when they interfered with the smooth functioning of authority.

17. This includes legislated restrictions of "free speech," from the Alien and Sedition Acts of the 18th century to the Espionage Act of World War

I; institutional powers such as the ability of governors or the president to declare martial law, or the emergency powers of FEMA and other agencies; and discretionary activities such as the surveillance and neutralization activities of the FBI under COINTELPRO or the USA PATRIOT Act.

18. Jennifer Steinhauer, "Just Keep It Peaceful, Protesters; New York Is Offering Discounts," New York Times, August 18, 2004, http://www. nytimes.com/2004/08/18/nyregion/18buttons.html?ex=1250481600& en=fab5ec7c870bb73a&ei=5090&partner=rssuserland.

19. Allan Dowd, "New Protests as Time Runs Out for WTO," The Herald (Glasgow), December 3, 1999, 14.

20. Cortright, "The Power of Nonviolence." I came across this article as a photocopy distributed and praised by a self-identified anarchist pacifist.

21. Churchill and Vander Wall, Agents of Repression, 281–284.

22. Ibid., 285.

23. Some might argue that a revolutionary movement that was misogynistic or racist could not use the right of self-determination as an excuse. The obvious counterarguments are that a) equating self-defense with misogyny or racism hardly amounts to a moral stance, and b) viewing violence as an immoral, chosen activity is simplistic and inaccurate. Submitting to the violence of oppression is at least as repugnant as killing one's oppressors (if our morality requires us to view killing enslavers as repugnant), and nonviolent privileged people benefit from, and are thus complicit in, the violence of oppression. Thus, the pretension that pacifists can justifiably condemn the violence of oppressed people with whom they might otherwise ally themselves is both silly and hypocritical.

24. Irwin and Faison, "Why Nonviolence?" 7, 9.

25. Cortright, "The Power of Nonviolence."

26. To read more on the evolution of the state's view of social control, see Williams, Our Enemies in Blue.

27. There were some minor instances of fighting back against police, but it was all in retreat. Anarchists had internalized the idea that only police could initiate violence, so if they did fight, it was only on the run. For a good compilation of information on the anti-FTAA protests in Miami, especially with regard to the traumatizing effects on many protestors, see The Miami Model: A Guide to the Events Surrounding the FTAA Ministerial in Miami, November 20–21, 2003 (Decentralized publication and distribution, 2003). For more information, write to theresonlynow@hotmail.com.

28. Wolfi Landstreicher, "Autonomous Self-Organization and Anarchist Intervention," *Anarchy: A Journal of Desire Armed*, no. 58 (Fall–Winter 2004): 56. The two following quotes in the paragraph are from the same page. Landstreicher recommends *Albania: Laboratory of Subversion* (London: Elephant Editions, 1999). Available online at http://www.endpage.com/Archives/Mirrors/Class_Against_Class/albania.html.

29. Fanon, *The Wretched of the Earth*, 124.

CHAPTER FOUR—NONVIOLENCE IS PATRIARCHAL

1. For more on patriarchy, I highly recommend the works of bell hooks, as well as Kate Bornstein (for example, *Gender Outlaw*) and Leslie Feinberg (for example, *Transgender Warriors*). Also, from a historical, anthropological approach, Gerda Lerner's *The Creation of Patriarchy* (New York: Oxford University Press, 1986) has good information, though Lerner largely limits herself to a binary perspective of gender, accepting two gender categories as natural, and thus missing the first and most important step in the creation of patriarchy, which is the creation of two rigid gender categories. Interesting information correcting this omission can be found in Moira Donald and Linda Hurcombe, eds., *Representations of Gender from Prehistory to Present* (New York: St. Martin's Press, 2000).

2. The latter strategy has been applied successfully by numerous anti-authoritarian societies throughout history, including the Igbo of present-day Nigeria. For that example, see Judith Van Allen, "'Sitting on a Man,' Colonialism and the Lost Political Institutions of Igbo Women," *Canadian Journal of African Studies*, vol. 2, (1972): 211–219.

3. For more on restorative justice, a "needs-based" form of dealing with social harm through healing and reconciliation (thus, a concept of justice suited for dealing with the many "crimes" that are rooted in patriarchy), see Larry Tifft, *Battering of Women: The Failure of Intervention and the Case for Prevention* (Boulder: Westview Press, 1993) and Dennis Sullivan and Larry Tifft, *Restorative Justice: Healing the Foundations of Our Everyday Lives* (Monsey, NY: Willow Tree Press, 2001).

4. bell hooks presents a more complex analysis, dealing also with the violence of women, in several books including *The Will to Change: Men, Masculinity, and Love* (New York: Atria Books, 2004). However, the women's violence that hooks discusses is not a political, conscious violence directed against the agents of patriarchy, but, rather, an impulsive displacement of abuse aimed at children and others lower in the social hierarchy. This is one example of a true cycle of violence, which pacifists assume to be the only form of violence. And while all

traumatic forms of violence cycle (that is, have successive ramifications as people maladaptively react to the trauma of the initial violence), revolutionary activists argue that all violent hierarchies are held together by systematic deployments of downward violence, the originators of which should and must be incapacitated. The world is not a level playing field on which violence rebounds consistently, evenly originating from and affecting people who are equal in power and responsibility. To be more specific, if women organized collectively to forcefully attack and oppose rapists, specific rapes would be prevented, the trauma of past rapes would be exorcised in a constructive and empowering way, men would be denied the option of raping with impunity, and future rapes would be discouraged. Or, for another example, urban blacks and Latinos who carry out guerrilla attacks against police would not encourage a cycle of police violence. Police do not kill people of color because they have been traumatized by past violence; they do so because the white supremacist system requires it and because they are paid to. Revolutionary activity will, of course, result in increased state repression, but that is an obstacle that must be surpassed in the destruction of the state, which is the greatest purveyor of violence. After the destruction of the state, of capitalism, and of patriarchal structures, people will still be traumatized, will still have authoritarian and patriarchal viewpoints, but individual problems that are not structurally reinforced can be addressed in cooperative, nonviolent ways. Armies cannot be.

5. For example, Robin Morgan, *The Demon Lover: On the Sexuality of Terrorism* (New York: W.W. Norton, 1989). The Rock Block Collective's pamphlet, *Stick it to the Manarchy* (Decentralized publication and distribution, 2001), makes valid criticisms against machismo in white anarchist circles, but suggests that militancy itself is macho, and that women, people of color, and other oppressed groups are somehow too fragile to participate in violent revolution.

6. Laina Tanglewood, "Against the Masculinization of Militancy," quoted in Ashen Ruins, *Against the Corpse Machine: Defining a Post-Leftist Anarchist Critique of Violence* (Decentralized publication and distribution, April 2002). Full text available at http://www.infoshop.org/rants/corpse_last.html.

7. Ibid.

8. Sue Daniels, e-mail, September 2004. For more on women's self-defense, Daniels recommends Martha McCaughey, *Real Knockouts: The Physical Feminism of Women's Self-Defense* (New York: New York University Press, 1997).

9. *The Will to Win! Women and Self-Defense* is an anonymous pamphlet distributed by Jacksonville Anarchist Black Cross (4204 Herschel Street, #20, Jacksonville, FL 32210).

10. The staid pacifist dictum that "change must come from within" is not to be confused with self-criticism. Functionally, such a philosophy only incapacitates people from challenging the system and fighting structural oppressions; it is analogous to the Christian notion of sin, as a barrier to rebellion and other collective action against oppression. In the few instances that the "change from within" principle means more than a simple commitment to nonviolence, it is an impotent form of self-improvement that pretends social oppressions are the result of widespread personality failures that can be overcome without the removal of external forces. The self-improvement of anti-oppression activists, on the other hand, is an admission that the external forces (that is, the structures of oppression) influence even those who fight against them. Thus, dealing with the effects is a fitting complement to fighting the causes. Rather than act as a complement, pacifist self-improvement tries to be a replacement.

11. "Be the change you wish to see in the world" or "Embody the change..." are common pacifist slogans that can be found on at least a couple of placards at any major peace protest in the US.

12. Personal e-mail to author, December 2003.

13. Cortright, "The Power of Nonviolence."

14. Robnett, *How Long?* 87, 166, 95.

15. The story of Bayard Rustin's having to leave the SCLC because Rustin was gay can be found in Jervis Andersen, *Bayard Rustin: The Troubles I've Seen* (New York: HarperCollins Publishers, 1997) and in David Dellinger, *From Yale to Jail: The Life Story of a Moral Dissenter* (New York: Pantheon Books, 1993).

16. However, people whose strategy relies on the formation of parties or similar centralized organizations, whether revolutionary or pacifist, also have an interest in muting self-criticism. But revolutionary activists of today demonstrate a marked trend away from political parties, unions, and other organizations that develop an ego, orthodoxy, and interest of their own.

17. Robnett, *How Long?* 93–96.

18. Abu-Jamal, *We Want Freedom,* 161.

19. Ibid., 159.

20. Ibid.

21. Julieta Paredes, "An Interview with Mujeres Creando," in *Quiet Rumours: An Anarcha-Feminist Reader*, ed. Dark Star Collective (Edinburgh: AK Press, 2002), 111–112.

22. Leslie Feinberg, "Leslie Feinberg Interviews Sylvia Rivera," *Workers World*, July 2, 1998, http://www.workers.org/ww/1998/sylvia0702.php.

23. Ann Hansen, *Direct Action: Memoirs of an Urban Guerrilla*, (Toronto: Between The Lines, 2002), 471.

24. Emma Goldman, "The Tragedy of Woman's Emancipation," in *Quiet Rumours*, ed. Dark Star Collective, 89.

25. Paul Avrich, *Anarchist Portraits* (Princeton: Princeton University Press, 1988), 218.

26. Yael, "Anna Mae Haunts the FBI," *Earth First! Journal*, July–August 2003: 51.

27. Ibid.

28. "Interview with Rote Zora," in *Quiet Rumours*, ed. Dark Star Collective, 102.

29. Ibid., 105.

30. For the sexism of the Weather Underground, see Tani and Sera, *False Nationalism*; and Dan Berger, *Outlaws of America: The Weather Underground and the Politics of Solidarity* (Oakland, CA: AK Press, 2005). For the Red Brigades' opposition to feminism, which they denounced wholesale as bourgeois rather than embracing its radical edges, see Chris Aronson Beck et al., *"Strike One to Educate One Hundred": The Rise of the Red Brigades in Italy in the 1960s–1970s* (Chicago: Seeds Beneath the Snow, 1986).

31. Carol Flinders, "Nonviolence: Does Gender Matter?" *Peace Power: Journal of Nonviolence and Conflict Transformation*, vol. 2, no. 2 (summer 2006); http://www.calpeacepower.org/0202/gender.htm. Flinders uses this exact example of Gandhi, even praising the innate pacifism of "devout Hindu wives."

32. Ibid.

33. For those unfamiliar with the term, something that is "gender-essentializing" assumes that gender is not a social construct or even a useful though imperfect division, but a set of inherent categories with unchanging and even deterministic essences.

34. Flinders, "Nonviolence: Does Gender Matter?"

35. Patrizia Longo, "Feminism and Nonviolence: A Relational Model," The Gandhi Institute, http://www.gandhiinstitute.org/NewsAndEvents/upload/nonviolence%20and%20relational%20feminism%20Memphis

%202004.pdf#search=%22feminist%20nonviolence%22.

36. "Feminism and Nonviolence Discussion," February and March 1998, http://www.h-net.org/~women/threads/disc-nonviolence.html (accessed October 18, 2006).

CHAPTER FIVE—NONVIOLENCE IS TACTICALLY & STRATEGICALLY INFERIOR

1. I have encountered this same formulation from at least three different nonviolent activists, including young environmentalists and old peace activists. I do not know if they all got the idea from a similar source or if they came up with it independently, but this glorification of capitulation certainly arises logically from their position.

2. Stephen Bender provides this extract from Bernays's book in his article "Propaganda, Public Relations, and the Not-So-New Dark Age," *LiP*, winter 2006: 25.

3. Ibid., 26.

4. For more on the propaganda theory of media, see Noam Chomsky and Edward Herman, *Manufacturing Consent: The Political Economy of the Mass Media* (New York: Pantheon Books, 1998) and Noam Chomsky, *Necessary Illusions* (Boston: South End Press, 1989). As the Iraqi insurgency grew in the months after President Bush declared major combat operations over, a number of CIA officials and Pentagon brass began defecting, publicly making statements that can be divided into three themes, all obviously centered around concerns of US hegemony: the invasion was poorly prepared, it is hurting our image abroad, or it is stretching our military to a breaking point.

5. Anyone familiar with independent media should know of several examples of both independent and pirate radio stations' being shut down by the FCC (as well as federal criminalization of independent radio in the last few years, leading to an expansion of what is considered "pirate"). For articles detailing individual cases of government repression of these radio stations see: "Pirate Radio Station Back On San Diego Airwaves," *Infoshop News*, January 6, 2006 and Emily Pyle, "The Death and Life of Free Radio," *The Austin Chronicle*, June 22, 2001. There is also the well-known fight between KPFA and Pacifica Radio, in which the corporate owner was the proxy repressor for the state.

6. Indymedia has been a primary target for this repression. The archive of the central Indymedia site (www.indymedia.org) probably contains the most comprehensive documentation of state repression of

various Indymedia sites across the globe. In the US, Sherman Austin, anarchist webmaster of the successful revolutionary site Raise the Fist, was imprisoned for one year on bogus charges. As of this writing, he is on probation and prohibited from using the internet. The federal government shut down his website.

7. Kalle Lasn's *Culture Jam* (New York: Quill, 2000) is flagrant in the reckless optimism with which it assumes that the dissemination of simple ideas can change society.

8. Unlike the state socialist media of the USSR, which enjoyed little credibility among its own cynical population, corporate media must be a total media system that enjoys the illusion of being above political propaganda. So if people on their way to work see a peaceful protest but hear nothing of that peaceful protest on the news, nothing is amiss. People outside the movement need little convincing that such a protest is irrelevant to them; thus, news editors can pretend they are responding to the demands of their audience. But if people on their way to work see a riot, or find out that a bomb has exploded outside a bank, and they can find no references to these occurrences in the mainstream media, they will be inclined to look elsewhere and to question what else the media is hiding. One of the reasons the corporate democratic system is a more effective totalitarian model than the one-party authoritarian state is that it has to respond to emergencies rather than ignore them.

9.Russian anarchists around the time of the 1905 revolution funded their massive propaganda drives and agitational leafletting with expropriations—armed robberies of the owning class. Paul Avrich, *The Russian Anarchists* (Oakland: AK Press, 2005), 44-48, 62. By combining education with militant tactics, otherwise impoverished people were able to buy printing presses and reach a mass audience with anarchist ideas.

10. John Tutino, *From Insurrection to Revolution in Mexico: Social Bases of Agrarian Violence, 1750-1940* (Princeton: Princeton University Press, 1986), 6.

11. Fanon, *The Wretched of the Earth*, 61.

12. More recently, SOAW has finally made some headway by working with Latin American regimes. Several Left-leaning governments in South America, namely Venezuela, Uruguay, and Argentina, agreed to stop sending soldiers and officers to the SOA. This is another example of pacifists having to rely on governments, which are coercive institutions, to accomplish their objectives. Specifically, they are dealing with governments that have challenged the "Washington Consensus"

and, thus, have less interest in getting their troops trained by the US. However, these governments have all been active in stomping on popular movements, by methods including suppressing dissident media and killing protestors. Because these governments have arisen from the authoritarian Left they have co-opted and fragmented rebellion. The end result is the same as when they were more closely aligned with Washington: control. It would also be useful to note that in some of these cases, notably in Argentina, militant social movements played a major role in toppling the prior US-aligned administrations and allowing the election of Leftist governments.

13. Beck et al., *"Strike One to Educate One Hundred,"* 190–193.

14. David Graeber, *Fragments of an Anarchist Anthropology* (Chicago: Prickly Paradigm Press, 2004). Anarchist and, not coincidentally, academic David Graeber suggests that, in addition to creating alternatives in the form of "international institutions" and "local and regional forms of self-governance," we should deprive states of their substance by removing "their capacity to inspire terror" (63). To accomplish this, he suggests that we "pretend nothing has changed, allow official state representatives to keep their dignity, even show up at their offices and fill out a form now and then, but otherwise, ignore them" (64). Curiously, he offers the vague examples of a couple of societies in Madagascar still dominated and exploited by neocolonial regimes as evidence that this pseudostrategy could somehow work.

15. Penny McCall-Howard, "Argentina's Factories: Now Producing Revolution," *Left Turn*, no. 7 (October/November 2002): http://www. leftturn.org/Articles/Viewer.aspx?id=308&type=M; and Michael Albert, "Argentine Self-Management," *ZNet*, November 3, 2005, http://www. zmag.org/content/showarticle.cfm?SectionID=26&ItemID=9042.

16. I do not wish to portray repression as an automatic thing. Sometimes the authorities do not notice something like an anarchist community center, and, more often, they choose to contain it rather than roll it back. But hard or soft, they do draw a line beyond which they will not let us pass without a fight.

17. Rick Rowley, *The Fourth World War* (Big Noise, 2003). Also see my critique of this film, *"The Fourth World War*: A Review," available on www. signalfire.org.

18. Ian Traynor, "US Campaign Behind the Turmoil in Kiev," *Guardian UK*, November 26, 2004, http://www.guardian.co.uk/international/ story/0,,1360080,00.html.

19. Williams, *Our Enemies in Blue*.

20. "Internal conflicts are another major source of vulnerability within the movement." Randy Borum and Chuck Tilby, "Anarchist Direct Actions: A Challenge for Law Enforcement," *Studies in Conflict and Terrorism*, no. 28 (2005): 219. The police themselves salivate over such backstabbing.

21. Quoted in *Fifth Estate*, no. 370 (fall 2005): 34.

22. George W. Bush, "Address to a Joint Session of Congress" (speech, United States Capitol, Washington, DC, September 20, 2001); http://www.whitehouse.gov/news/releases/2001/09/20010920-8.html.

23. At the time of this writing, more than a dozen alleged members of the Earth Liberation Front (ELF) and the Animal Liberation Front (ALF) have been arrested after the FBI infiltrated the radical environmental movement. They have been threatened with life sentences for simple arsons, and, under this tremendous pressure, many have agreed to snitch for the government. Six activists with Stop Huntingdon Animal Cruelty (SHAC), a group that waged a successful and aggressive boycott against a company that tested on animals, were charged in March 2006 under the Animal Enterprise Terrorism Act and recently imprisoned for several years. Rodney Coronado, a longtime environmental and indigenous activist and former ELF prisoner, was just sent back to prison merely for giving a workshop that encouraged radical environmentalism and included information about how he built the incendiary device used in the attack for which he was already imprisoned.

24. Williams, *Our Enemies in Blue*, 201.

25. JH, "World War I: The Chicago Trial," *Fifth Estate*, no. 370 (fall 2005): 24.

26. JH, "Sabotage," *Fifth Estate*, no. 370 (fall 2005): 22.

27. JH, "World War I: The Chicago Trial," 24.

28. Paul Avrich, *Sacco and Vanzetti: The Anarchist Background* (Princeton: Princeton University Press, 1991), 153, 165.

29. The Galleanists were a group of anarchists centered around a paper published by Luigi Galleani. Though they were influenced by Galleani's brand of anarchism, they did not appoint him leader or actually name themselves after him. The label "Galleanist" is primarily one of convenience.

30. Paul Avrich, *Sacco and Vanzetti: The Anarchist Background*, 127.

31. Ibid., 207.

32. Ibid., 127.

33. Ibid., 147.

34. Ibid., 209.

35. Ibid., 211.

36. Ibid., 213.

37. Lon Savage, *Thunder in the Mountains: The West Virginia Mine War, 1920–21* (Pittsburgh: University of Pittsburgh Press, 1990).

38. Borum and Tilby, "Anarchist Direct Actions," 220.

39. As of January 2006, 88 percent of Sunnis in Iraq and 41 percent of Shiites admit that they approve of attacks on US-led forces (*Editor & Publisher*, "Half of Iraqis Back Attacks on US," reprinted in *Asheville Global Report*, no. 369 [February 9–15, 2006]: http://www.agrnews.org/?section=archives&cat_id=13&section_id=10&briefs=true). It is possible that, given the climate of political repression in Iraq, the actual percentages are higher but many did not wish to disclose their support for the insurgency to pollsters. In August 2005, 82 percent of Iraqis said they "strongly oppose" the presence of occupation troops, according to a secret British military poll that was leaked to the press. The same percentage reported that they wanted US troops out of their country in a May 2004 poll taken by the Coalition Provisional Authority (Thomas E. Ricks, "82 Percent of Iraqis Oppose US Occupation," *Washington Post* (May 13, 2004): http://www.globalpolicy.org/ngos/advocacy/protest/iraq/2004/0513poll.htm. However, these days it is hard to talk about an Iraqi resistance, because Western media coverage would have us believe the only thing going on is the sectarian bombing of civilians. The strong possibility exists that these bombings are orchestrated by the occupiers, though from our current vantage we really cannot know what is going on in the resistance. Suffice it to say, most Iraqi resistance groups have taken a position against killing civilians, and it is to these groups that I refer. I wrote more on the possibility of US involvement in sectarian killings in "An Anarchist Critique of the Iraq War," available on www.signalfire.org.

40. Martin Oppenheimer, *The Urban Guerrilla* (Chicago: Quadrangle Books, 1969), 141–142.

CHAPTER SIX—NONVIOLENCE IS DELUDED

1. Michael Nagler, *The Steps of Nonviolence* (New York: The Fellowship of Reconciliation, 1999), Introduction. Anything other than nonviolence is portrayed to be the result of "fear and anger...potentially damaging emotions."

2. Irwin and Faison, "Why Nonviolence?"

3. Ibid.

4. Tani and Sera, *False Nationalism*, 167.

5. George Jackson, *Blood In My Eye* (Baltimore: Black Classics Press, 1990).

6. Abu-Jamal, *We Want Freedom*, 105.

7. Kuwasi Balagoon, *A Soldier's Story: Writings of a Revolutionary New Afrikan Anarchist* (Montreal: Solidarity, 2001), 28, 30, 72.

8. Fanon, *The Wretched of the Earth*, 249–251.

9. "Active resistance occurs when activists use force against the police... or proactively engage in illegal activity such as vandalism, sabotage, or property damage." This sentence appears in Borum and Tilby, "Anarchist Direct Actions," 211. The authors, one a professor and one a former police chief, include sit-ins and the like as passive resistance.

10. I am referring to the black bloc as a militant tactic, not to punk fashion blocs that wear all black but in the end act passively. Real black blocs are becoming less common in the US.

11. Spruce Houser, "Violence/Nonviolence" panel discussion. Houser is a self-proclaimed anarchist and pacifist.

12. Houser, "Domestic Anarchist Movement Increasingly Espouses Violence," http://athensnews.com/index.php?action=viewarticle&section=archives&story_id=17497. In true pacifist form, Houser submitted his article to the Athens News in preparation for the coming North American Anarchist Conference, in an attempt to bolster pacifism by turning local public opinion against the "violent anarchists." He meekly protests the fact that his article was turned by the corporate media into propaganda against the entire anarchist movement with a handwritten note, scrawled on the many photocopies of the article he handed out, stating that his original title was "Anarchism and Violence," but the editor changed it.

13. Burt Green, "The Meaning of Tiananmen," *Anarchy: A Journal of Desire Armed*, no. 58 (Fall–Winter 2004): 44.

14. Judith Kohler, "Antiwar Nuns Sentenced to 2 1/2 Years," Associated Press, July 25, 2003. I won't begrudge anyone the use of any trial strategy she deems appropriate, but, in this case, the nuns' argument truthfully reflects the fact that they did not cause any real, physical destruction to the missile facility, when they certainly had an opportunity to cause such destruction.

15. A third possible definition might try to draw a line, based on common sense, through the potential candidates for violence. If we lived in a needs-based political economy, common sense would recognize people's need to defend themselves and live free of oppression; thus, revolutionary action toward the goal of a society in which everyone could achieve their needs could not be considered violent. Because we live in a society in which our concept of justice is based on punishment, which is to say that the behavior of just people is the avoidance of transgression, common sense recognizes paying taxes (to an imperialist state) to be nonviolent, while paying a contract killer is considered violent. Though both actions have similar results, it is certainly easier to expect people not to commit the latter action (which requires taking initiative) and permit them to commit the former action (which is just going along with the flow). In such a society (for example, ours), pacifism really is passivism because not committing violence really has more to do with avoiding culpability than with taking responsibility.

16. Todd Allin Morman, "Revolutionary Violence and the Future Anarchist Order," *Social Anarchism*, no. 38 (2005): 30–38.

17. Ibid., 34.

18. Ibid., 35.

19. Fanon, *The Wretched of the Earth*, 306.

20. Churchill and Vander Wall, *Agents of Repression*, 103–106.

21. This is what academic anarchist Howard Ehrlich advised in his keynote address to the North American Anarchist Convergence in Athens, Ohio, August 14, 2004.

22. Quoted in a video clip included in Sam Green and Bill Siegel, director/producer, *The Weather Underground* (The Free History Project, 2003). As for the flexibility of Gandhi's commitment to nonviolence, his words on Palestinian resistance are informative: "I wish they had chosen the way of non-violence in resisting what they rightly regard as an unacceptable encroachment upon their country. But according to the accepted canons of right and wrong, nothing can be said against the Arab resistance in the face of overwhelming odds." Jews for Justice in the Middle East, *The Origin of the Palestine-Israel Conflict*, 3rd ed. (Berkeley: Jews for Justice in the Middle East, 2001). The authors cite Martin Buber and Paul R. Mendes-Flohr, *A Land of Two Peoples* (New York: Oxford University Press, 1983).

23. Nonviolent activists frequently rely on the media to disseminate their point. I have already mentioned multiple examples involving protests. For another example: On January 31, 2006, an activist on a listserv for the supposedly radical anti-authoritarian group Food Not Bombs posted

a suggestion for an action during President Bush's State of the Union address. The suggestion was for thousands of people to Google the phrase "Impeach Bush" during his speech. Supposedly, the corporate media would pick up on this factoid and begin publicizing it rather than their typical surface analysis of how well Bush presented himself in his speech. Needless to say, no such thing occurred.

24. Malcolm X had this to say about Gandhian notions of universal brotherhood and love: "My belief in brotherhood would never restrain me in any way from protecting myself in a society from a people whose disrespect for brotherhood makes them feel inclined to put my neck on a tree at the end of a rope." Perry, *Malcolm X: The Last Speeches*, 88.

25. For example, my acquaintances in prison were quite conservative in condemning the "DC Sniper" and even hoping that the perpetrator would get the death penalty. But when an off-duty FBI agent was added to the list of sniper victims, they all expressed immense satisfaction.

26. Ashen Ruins, *Against the Corpse Machine.*

27. A prime example is Stephen Salisbury and Mark Fineman, "Deep Down at Graterford: Jo-Jo Bowen and 'The Hole,'" *The Philadelphia Inquirer*, vol. 305, no. 131, November 8, 1981, A1. The first six paragraphs of the article are all about Joseph Bowen and his experiences in the Hole, including numerous quotes from Bowen and personalizing descriptions that portray him as he speaks—the reader is thus brought into the prison right next to him. The eighth paragraph begins, "But Joseph Bowen also forced those negotiators—and, thus, the world on the streets outside—to see more than a three-time murderer with new-found power. Through negotiator Chuck Stone and the media that covered every nuance of his five-day siege, Bowen also forced the outside world to confront the realities of another world—a world of institutions he and thousands of other inmates in Pennsylvania perceive as oppressive and racist, robbing human beings of not only their dignity, but, sometimes, their lives."

28. Churchill, *Pacifism as Pathology*, 70–75.

29. To confirm the prevalence of this mindset among anti-SOA pacifists, and to hear these preposterous claims repeated ad nauseam, one need only attend the yearly vigil outside Fort Benning, home of the SOA.

30. Eating meat and paying taxes are perhaps self-explanatory. Research into aluminum production (and the concomitant of hydro-electric dam construction), auto-factory conditions, air pollution caused by internal combustion engines, the level of fatalities incurred as a matter of course by a car culture, and the way in which industrialized nations procure their

petroleum will reveal why driving a car is a violent activity, enough so that we cannot take seriously a moral pacifist who drives a car. Eating tofu, in the current economy, is integrally connected to the use of disposable immigrant labor, genetic modifications of soy and the resulting destruction of ecosystems and food cultures, and the ability of the United States to undermine subsistence-farming cultures around the world, fueling globalization with the threat and reality of starvation. Paying rent supports property owners who will throw a family out into the streets if they cannot make payments in time, who invest in ecocidal development and urban sprawl, and who assist in the gentrifying of cities, with attendant violence levied against homeless people, people of color, and low-income families. Being nice to a cop contributes to the masochist culture of worship that allows agents of law and order to beat and murder people with impunity. It is a striking historical peculiarity that allows police to enjoy broad popular support, and even think of themselves as heroes, when it used to be that they were well known as scum and lackeys of the ruling class.

31. Fanon, *The Wretched of the Earth*, 54.

32. "We are at war...." Art Burton (keynote address, People United, Afton, VA, June 19, 2004). Burton was a member of the Richmond NAACP. The Zapatistas describe the current world order as the Fourth World War, and this sentiment has been echoed across the globe.

CHAPTER SEVEN—THE ALTERNATIVE

1. Helen Woodson and my former codefendant and cellmate Jerry Zawada come to mind as committed, pacifist revolutionaries.

2. Though this particular quote is my own wording, the argument it represents comes frequently from the mouths of nonviolent activists. Todd Allin Morman begins his article "Revolutionary Violence and the Future Anarchist Order" by pointing out that none of the violent revolutions in the United States, Russia, China, or Cuba "has led to a just society, a free society or even to a 'workers' paradise'" (30).

3. I am judging the Leninists' motivations by the aims and actions of their leaders—as members of an authoritarian organization, the rank-and-file demonstrably prioritized following the leaders over their own intentions, good or bad. The aims and actions of the Leninist leadership, from the very beginning, included improving and expanding the Tsarist secret police, reconstituted as the Cheka; forcibly converting millions of independent peasants into wage laborers; blocking direct barter between producers; instituting stark wage hierarchies between officers and soldiers in the military, which was composed largely of ex-Tsarist officers; taking

over, centralizing, and ultimately destroying the independent workers' "soviets," or councils; seeking and accepting development loans from British and American capitalists; bargaining and collaborating with imperialist powers at the end of World War I; repressing the activism and publications of anarchists and social revolutionaries; and more. See Alexander Berkman, *The Bolshevik Myth* (London: Freedom Press, 1989), Alexandre Skirda, *Nestor Makhno, Anarchy's Cossack: The Struggle for Free Soviets in the Ukraine 1917–1921* (Oakland: AK Press, 2004), and Voline, *The Unknown Revolution* (Montreal: Black Rose, 2004).

4. A good history of this movement can be found in Alexandre Skirda, *Nestor Makhno, Anarchy's Cossack*.

5. In their article written for police strategists, "Anarchist Direct Actions," Randy Borum and Chuck Tilby point out that in some cases decentralization has left anarchists isolated and more vulnerable to repression, though on the whole it is clear that decentralization makes radical groups harder to infiltrate and repress; communication, coordination, and solidarity are the critical components for the survival of decentralized networks. Borum and Tilby, "Anarchist Direct Actions," 203–223.

6. Without autonomy, there can be no freedom. For a basic introduction to these and other anarchist principles, see Errico Malatesta, *Anarchy* (London: Freedom Press, 1920); or Peter Kropotkin, *Mutual Aid: A Factor in Evolution* (New York: Alfred A. Knopf, 1921). A good article containing thoughts on an anarchist revolutionary process similar to the one I have phrased is Wolfi Landstreicher's "Autonomous Self-Organization and Anarchist Intervention." Also, Roger White's *Post Colonial Anarchism* provides a number of important arguments for the right of each community and nation to autonomously identify itself and choose its method of struggle.

7. For example, the Black Liberation Army, one of the more successful urban guerrilla groups in the US, failed in large part for want of an above-ground support structure, according to Jalil Muntaqim, *We Are Our Own Liberators* (Montreal: Abraham Guillen Press, 2002), 37–38. On the other hand, the anarchist insurgent army led by Makhno in Ukraine could sustain effective guerrilla warfare against the immensely larger and better-armed Red Army for so long precisely because it enjoyed a great deal of support from the peasantry, who hid and tended wounded insurgents, provided food and supplies, and collected information on enemy positions. Skirda, *Makhno, Anarchy's Cossack*, 248, 254–255.

8. John Sayles, "Foreword," in Lon Savage's *Thunder in the Mountains: The West Virginia Mine War, 1920–21* (Pittsburgh: University of Pittsburgh Press, 1990).

i

INDEX

| 171 |

Mumia Abu-Jamal, *We Want Freedom: A Life in the Black Panther Party.* South End Press, 2004.

Antonio Antonius, *Arab Awakening.* 1938 (Simon Publications, 2001).

Jimmy Santiago Baca, *A Place to Stand: The Making of Poet.* Grove Press, 2001.

r

Kuwasi Balagoon, *A Soldier's Story: Writings of a Revolutionary New Afrikan Anarchist.* Solidarity, 2001.

Gioconda Belli, *The Country Under My Skin: A Memoir of Love and War.* Knopf, 2002.

RECOMMENDED

R E A D I N G

Dee Brown, *Bury My Heart at Wounded Knee: An Indian History of the American West.* Arena, 1987.

Stuart Christie, *Granny Made Me an Anarchist.* Scribner, 2004.

Ward Churchill, *Agents of Repression: The FBI's Secret Wars Against the Black Panther Party and the American Indian Movement.* South End Press, 2002.

——*Pacifism as Pathology.* Arbeiter Ring, 1998.

Dark Star Collective, *Quiet Rumors: An Anarcha-Feminist Reader.* AK Press, 2002.

Frantz Fanon, *The Wretched of the Earth.* Grove, 1963 (2005).

Denise Giardina, *Storming Heaven.* Ballantine Books, 1987.

David Gilbert, *No Surrender: Writings of an Anti-Imperialist PoliticalPrisoner.* Abraham Guillen Press, 2004.

Ann Hansen, *Direct Action: Memoirs of an Urban Guerrilla.* Between the Lines, 2002.

Subcommandante Insurgente Marcos, *Our Word is Our Weapon.* Seven Stories Press, 2001.

Martha McCaughey, *Real Knockouts: The Physical Feminism of Women's Self-Defense.* New York University Press, 1997.

The Network for Asian Liberation, *Selected Writings from the Frontlines.*

George Orwell, *Homage to Catalonia.* Harcourt, Brace, & World, 1952.

Ashen Ruins, *Against the Corpse Machine: Defining a Post-Leftist Anarchist Critique of Violence.* Stolen Press, 2002.

Assata Shakur, *Assata: An Autobiography.* Lawrence Hill, 1987.

Alexandre Skirda, *Nestor Makhno, Anarchy's Cossack: The Struggle for Free Soviets in the Ukraine 1917-1921.* AK Press, 2004.

Robert Williams, *Negroes With Guns.* 1962 (Wayne State University Press, 1998).

ABOUT SOUTH END PRESS

South End Press is an independent, collectively run book publisher with more than 250 titles in print. Since our founding in 1977, we have met the needs of readers who are exploring, or are already committed to, the politics of radical social change. We publish books that encourage critical thinking and constructive action on the key political, cultural, social, economic, and ecological issues shaping life in the United States and in the world. We provide a forum for a wide variety of democratic social movements and an alternative to the products of corporate publishing.

From its inception, South End has organized itself as an egalitarian collective with decision-making arranged to share as equally as possible the rewards and stresses of running the business. Each collective member is responsible for core editorial and administrative tasks, and all collective members earn the same base salary. South End also has made a practice of inverting the pervasive racial and gender hierarchies in traditional publishing houses; our collective has been majority women since the mid-1980s, and at least 50 percent people of color since the mid-1990s.

Our author list—which includes bell hooks, Andrea Smith, Arundhati Roy, Noam Chomsky, Winona LaDuke, Manning Marable, Ward Churchill, Cherríe Moraga, and Howard Zinn—reflects South End's commitment to publish on myriad issues from diverse perspectives. Learn more at www.southendpress.org

Peter Gelderloos is a radical community organizer from Virginia. He is the author of *Consensus: A New Handbook for Grassroots Political, Social, and Environmental Groups* and a contributor to *Letters From Young Activists: Today's Rebels Speak Out.* He has also authored several pamphlets, including *What Is Democracy?* and *World Behind Bars.*

After serving a six month prison sentence for an illegal nonviolent protest at Ft. Benning with SOA Watch, Peter Gelderloos became involved in prisoner support and anti-prison organizing. He co-facilitates workshops on the prison system and prison abolition. In addition to participating in the anti-globalization and anti-war movements as a demonstrator, organizer, and journalist, Gelderloos has been active with Harrisonburg's Rising Up Collective, as well as the local Food Not Bombs, Copwatch, and Anarchist Black Cross chapters. He helped start two anarchist community centers in Harrisonburg, Virginia—the 181 Collective Space, and, after the authorities shut that one down, the Rocktown Infoshop, which is still open.

For Peter Gelderloos's latest writing visit www.signalfire.org

ABOUT THE AUTHOR

COMMUNITY SUPPORTED PUBLISHING
Celebrate the bounty of the harvest! Community Supported Agriculture (CSA) is helping to make independent, healthy farming sustainable. Now there is Community Supported Publishing (CSP)! By joining the South End Press CSP you ensure a steady crop of books guaranteed to change your world. As a member you receive one the new varieties or a choice heirloom selection free each month and a 10% discount on everything else. Subscriptions start at $20/month. Email southend@southendpress.org for more information.